NFL's GREATEST

PRO FOOTBALL'S BEST PLAYERS, TEAMS, AND GAMES

Text by
PHIL BARBER *and* JOHN FAWAZ

Foreword by
STEVE SABOL

A Dorling Kindersley Book

IN ASSOCIATION WITH THE NATIONAL FOOTBALL LEAGUE
NFL Properties Publishing Group

Dorling **DK** Kindersley
LONDON, NEW YORK, SYDNEY, DELHI, PARIS,
MUNICH and JOHANNESBURG

NFL Publishing
Editor-in-Chief John Wiebusch
General Manager Bill Barron
Managing Editor Chuck Garrity, Sr.
NFL's Greatest **Editor** Tom Barnidge
Executive Art Director Brad Jansen
NFL's Greatest **Art Director** Bill Madrid
Director–Photo Services Paul Spinelli
Photo Editor Kevin Terrell
Manager-Photo Services Tina Resnick
Director–Manufacturing Dick Falk
Director–Print Services Tina Dahl
Manager–Computer Graphics Sandy Gordon
Publishing Director Bob O'Keefe
Publishing Manager Lori Quenneville

DORLING KINDERSLEY
Publisher Sean Moore
Editorial Director LaVonne Carlson
Art Directors Dirk Kaufman, Tina Vaughan

First American Edition, 2000
10 9 8 7 6 5 4 3 2 1

Published in the United States by
Dorling Kindersley Publishing, Inc.
95 Madison Avenue
New York, New York 10016

Copyright © 2000
Dorling Kindersley Publishing Limited
and National Football League Properties, Inc.

NFL's greatest : pro football's best players, teams, and
games. -- 1st American ed.
"In association with the National Football League."
ISBN 0-7894-5955-8

1. National Football League Publishing. I. DK Publishing,
Inc. II. National Football League. III. Title: Pro football's best
players, teams, and games.

Produced by National Football League Properties, Inc.
Publishing Division
6701 Center Drive West, Suite 1111
Los Angeles, California 90045

Printed and bound in Portugal in Printer Portuguesa

DK Publishing books are available at special discounts for bulk
purchases for sales promotions or premiums. Special editions,
including personalized covers, excerpts of existing guides, and
corporate imprints can be created in large quantities for specific
needs. For more information, contact Special Markets Dept./
DK Publishing, Inc./95 Madison Avenue/New York, New York 10016/
FAX: 800-600-9098

see our complete catalog at
www.dk.com

CONTENTS

FOREWORD BY STEVE SABOL

*1968: The Jets'
only world
championship*

100 GREATEST PLAYERS OF ALL TIME

*Steelers star
Terry Bradshaw*

*Elroy
(Crazylegs)
Hirsch*

*NFL career receiving
leader Jerry Rice*

Cowboys star
Troy Aikman

25 GREATEST TEAMS OF ALL TIME
92

Super Bowl
VII coin

1972 Dolphins: NFL's only perfect team

"Greatest Game
Ever Played"

Bronko
Nagurski

25 MOST IMPORTANT EVENTS
142

Legendary Packers
coach Vince Lombardi

The first
professional
player

25 GREATEST GAMES OF ALL TIME
120

Commissioner
Pete Rozelle

Ball commemorating
the 1958 title game.

1974: Raiders end Miami's reign

THE ACID TEST OF GREATNESS

BY STEVE SABOL

What would we give for the opportunity to behold, in person, a gallop by Red Grange, a power sweep by Lombardi's Packers, a sideline pass from Unitas to Berry, or a quarterback sack by Deacon Jones, the man who coined the expression? Oh, to be able to say of Hutson, or Baugh, or Van Buren, *I saw him play*. In a way, those four little words are the acid test of who is great and who isn't.

Walsh's 49ers, the Monsters of the Midway, Dallas's Doomsday Defense. *I saw them play*. Those words connote both privilege and reverence. Does the phrase fit Jim Brown? Of course. Lance Alworth? You bet.

Profiled in these pages are 100 players and 25 teams deserving of those words. They were chosen by members of the Pro Football Hall of Fame Selection Committee. Einstein didn't create a theory for this one. There's no formula, no equation to determine the greatest players, the greatest teams, and the greatest games in the history of the NFL. Everyone has an opinion. I have my favorites, and almost all of them appear in this book.

Each of the great teams had its own signature. The 1975 Steelers were thoroughbreds. The 1950 Browns meant talent. The 1989 49ers were ritzy, dapper, and disciplined. The 1972 Dolphins meant brains. Then there are the Super Bowl Shufflin' Bears, whose 1985 season stands as the most sustained work of defensive devastation ever committed on a football field by any team, anywhere, any time. They were like a musical group that had one monster hit then disappeared, like the Rays singing "Silhouettes."

The Bears achieved greatness because of the perfection of their skills, the 1966 Packers because of the persistence of their will. *Lombardi's Packers*. There's a phrase that stands by itself in the lexicon of football, connoting mountaintop greatness. They were the Romans of the sport—triumphal, imperial, surrounded by an aura of the certainty of victory. Starr, Davis, Taylor, Hornung, Adderley, Nitschke. Names that raise the hair on the back of the neck of any serious fan. Nine members of Lombardi's Packers are in the Pro Football Hall of Fame. That's the most of any team in league history. Yet, no one from the 1966 Packers made the *NFL's Greatest All-Time Team!* Not even Forrest Gregg, whom Lombardi described as "the greatest player I ever coached."

Vince's ghost will arise and slime us for that!

I also would have selected New York's Mel Hein as my All-Time center. He was a 60-minute regular for 15 years, an all-pro for eight consecutive years, and a charter member of the Hall of Fame. I'm glad Walter Payton was chosen for the

All-Time Team. My son Casey tells everyone how I held him up in front of the television and told him to watch number 34 of the Bears. I remember telling him at the time that years from now, you'll be able to tell your friends, *I saw him play*.

My all-time favorite player, Dick Butkus, was another member of the Chicago Bears who was selected to our All-Time Team. There were many Sunday afternoons when I had the privilege of watching Butkus play from my sideline camera position at Wrigley Field. If you blindfolded me, I still could tell you when Butkus made a tackle. It had a special crunch. In the Bears' 1967 highlight film, I described him as "Moby Dick in a goldfish bowl." He was a force of unimaginable proportions. He just didn't tackle ball carriers. He ravaged, mauled, and brutalized them. Anything that was loose—a chin-strap, an elbow pad, a shoelace—was ripped off.

Talk to anyone who played in the NFL during the late 1960s, and he'll tell you that part of the stature that he enjoyed as a pro player came from

Forrest Gregg: Lombardi's favorite player

having faced Dick Butkus. John Brodie told me that before every football season he would have a recurring nightmare. He dreamed he was playing naked, and every player on the opposing team was Dick Butkus.

A book on the greatest teams and players would be enough on its own, but our panel also has selected the 25 greatest games and pro football's 25 most important events. In the latter category, I would add a twenty-sixth—the signing of the NFL's television contract on October 12, 1977. When the television networks (ABC, CBS, and NBC) agreed to pay $656 million for the NFL's TV rights, it not only was the largest television package ever negotiated but it was the first time the league made more money from television than from ticket sales. That event stands out as one of the most significant in the growth of the game.

Twenty of the Greatest Games are playoff or championship games, which reinforces one of the most revered sporting axioms: Cherish your toughest opponent because he raises you to a higher level. To me, a great game must have the pacing of a good book. It must have an intriguing beginning, some twists and turns in the plot during the middle, and a dramatic, if not surprising ending. So I was pleased to see that our panel included the 1974 playoff battle between the Raiders and the Dolphins. What a mind-bending, heart-rending, digestion-ending, see-saw struggle that was. It was decided in the final seconds when Ken Stabler flicked a desperation toss into "a sea of hands" in the end zone and Clarence Davis outfought three Dolphins defenders to secure the pass and a 28-26 victory for Oakland.

A game that could be added to a list of the greatest is the 1933 NFL Championship Game—the first one. The Bears defeated the Giants 23-21 in a game in which the lead changed hands six times and the winning touchdown was scored on a trick play. Bronko Nagurski threw a pass to Bill Hewitt, who lateraled to Bill Karr, who raced the last 19 yards to give Chicago the victory in the NFL's first official title game.

There is magic in the game of football. This book is about the men who have created, conveyed, and possessed this magic. The photographs here bring us face to face with those young men of long ago, of yesterday, and of today, enabling us to see once more how they elevated their game—and all of sports—to astonishing heights. They left their footprints on football's highest peaks.

And now those indelible footprints are there to be followed by today's stars such as Terrell Davis, Brett Favre, Jevon Kearse, and Keyshawn Johnson. Years from now, someone will say *I saw them play*.

100
GREATEST
PLAYERS
OF ALL TIME

WINNING WAYS
During Herb Adderley's nine seasons with the Green Bay Packers and three with the Dallas Cowboys, the two clubs had a composite regular-season record of 119-44-5 (.723) and earned eight playoff berths.

HERB ADDERLEY

Cornerback
Green Bay (1961-69)
Dallas (1970-72)

The 200-pound Adderley was a very physically intimidating presence in man-for-man coverage. "Herb Adderley was able to play receivers as close as anyone in the league because he had so much speed," said Norb Hecker, his defensive backfield coach in Green Bay.

Adderley's speed was good for more than defense. He was a thrilling open-field runner who averaged 25.7 yards on 120 kickoff returns, including a 103-yard touchdown in 1962. He was just as dangerous after intercepting passes, averaging 21.8 yards on 48 career returns, including 7 touchdowns.

Legendary Green Bay Packers coach Vince Lombardi did not make many mistakes. When he did, he was big enough to admit them.

"When I think of what [Herb] Adderley means to our defense," Lombardi once said, "it scares me to remember how I mishandled him."

Drafted as a running back, Adderley really wanted to play cornerback. After a lackluster half-season in the backfield, Lombardi finally conceded his mistake. Years later, quarterback Bart Starr would call Adderley "the greatest cornerback ever to play this game."

Adderley's running abilities took center stage in Super Bowl II. With the Packers leading the Oakland Raiders 26-7 in the fourth quarter, he stepped in front of wide receiver Fred Biletnikoff and intercepted a pass from Daryle Lamonica. Sixty yards later, Adderley had the first interception return for a touchdown in Super Bowl history, and the Packers had wrapped up a victory in Lombardi's final game with Green Bay. His 60-yard return remained a Super Bowl record until 1977.

Adderley played on five NFL championship teams and two Super Bowl winners with the Packers. After joining the Dallas Cowboys late in his career, he added two more Super Bowl appearances, including a 24-3 victory over Miami in game VI.

When Adderley was inducted into the Pro Football Hall of Fame in 1980, he had an interesting observation: "I'm not sure, but I'd be willing to bet my winning percentage is as high as anybody who ever played this game."

LANCE ALWORTH

Wide Receiver
San Diego (1962-1970)
Dallas (1971-72)

At the height of the AFL-NFL war during the 1960s, traditionalists chided the junior league for its seeming lack of defense. Chiefs owner Lamar Hunt, one of the AFL's founders, had his own theory about how that criticism might have originated.

"I think what happened is that the NFL watched a lot of Lance Alworth's highlight films," Hunt said. "He made it look like a wide-open game because he was always open."

Indeed, during nine seasons with the Chargers and, to a lesser extent, two more with Dallas, Alworth was head and shoulders above the crowd—literally and poetically. Alworth's nickname was "Bambi," a name for which he never cared, but it did reflect his leaping, floating, acrobatic style.

"I've never seen an end who could run down the field, time his leap, and jump as high as Lance to catch balls," said Sid Gillman, his coach in San Diego.

Alworth rarely caught a pass as a halfback at Arkansas. Limited by a muscle tear, he had only 10 receptions as a Chargers' rookie in 1962. But he soon became the AFL's marquee player. He had more than 1,000 receiving yards every year from 1963-69, and he scored 42 touchdowns from 1964-66. His career numbers include 542 receptions for 10,266 yards and 85 touchdowns, and his 18.9-yard average ranks second among players with 500 or more catches.

In 1978, Alworth's genius was recognized when he became the first AFL player to enter the Pro Football Hall of Fame.

"He is the best wide receiver I've ever seen," said long-time announcer Charlie Jones. "He had speed, quickness, and toughness. When I envision one of those photographs of the mind, I see him airborne—like a ballet dancer—reaching back for the pass."

Charley Hennigan, a star wide receiver for the Houston Oilers, may have put it best: "A player comes along once in a lifetime who alone is worth the price of admission. Lance Alworth was that player."

LEM BARNEY
Cornerback
Detroit (1967-1977)

In the opening game of the 1967 season, Bart Starr, the quarterback of the NFL-champion Packers, figured he'd pick on a rookie defender. He lofted a pass over the head of Lem Barney, a cornerback from unheralded Jackson State. Barney caught the pass over his shoulder, somersaulted, regained his footing, and returned it 24 yards for a touchdown. He finished the year with 10 interceptions and 3 touchdowns.

Barney was named NFL defensive player of the year and selected for the Pro Bowl. The secret was out.

"He's unbelievable," former Lions coach Joe Schmidt said of Barney. "No matter what he's asked to do for us, he does it in spectacular fashion. I wish I had two others just like him. I'd play one next to him on defense and I'd use the other on offense."

Often, it must have seemed to opponents as if there were more than one Lem Barney on the football field.

He intercepted 56 passes in his career, but that doesn't speak to his versatility. Barney scored 11 touchdowns—7 on interception returns, 2 on punt returns, 1 on a kickoff return, and another on the return of a missed field goal. He also recovered 11 opponents' fumbles and doubled as the Lions' punter in 1967 and 1969.

"I enjoyed the challenges of picking one off and taking it in for a score," Barney said. "And I enjoyed making the big tackle to stop a first-down try, knocking a pass down to keep a drive from staying alive, returning a punt, returning a kickoff, trying to set the offense up in good field position, doing whatever I could to contribute to a victory."

One memorable performance against the Packers in the last regular-season game of the 1970 season illustrates this point. The versatile Barney had a 74-yard kickoff return, a 65-yard punt return, and a 49-yard interception return, either scoring or setting up all of the Lions' points in a 20-0 victory.

Barney played in seven Pro Bowls and was named all-pro in 1968 and 1969.

"The game was fun for me," Barney said. "I whistled while I worked."

SAMMY BAUGH

Quarterback
Washington (1937-1952)

The man who united the changes was Slingin' Sammy Baugh, the NFL's first great quarterback.

The wiry Texan (6 feet 2 inches, 180 pounds) completed 11 of 16 passes in his first NFL game, and finished his rookie year by zipping 3 long touchdown passes to lead the Redskins to a 28-21 victory over the Bears in the 1937 NFL Championship Game.

That season, pro football woke up to the possibilities of the aerial game. "They finally realized that people liked to see scoring," Baugh explained. "You don't want to sit out there in the cold and see a fourteen-to-six game."

There weren't many low-scoring games when Slingin' Sam had the ball. He led the NFL in passing six times, three times after making the switch to the T-formation in 1944. Baugh led the Redskins to five division titles and two NFL championships in his first nine seasons, and he became an enormous box-office draw.

He was more than just an arm. In an era when players performed on both offense and defense, Baugh was an accomplished safety (31 career interceptions) and a terrific punter who established still-existing records for highest average in a season (51.4 yards in 1940) and a career (45.1 yards). Baugh won a rare "triple crown" in 1943, leading the NFL in passing, punting, and interceptions. In fact, the six-time all-league selection led the NFL in punting four consecutive years, 1940-43.

But it is his passing for which he is best remembered. In 1947, he passed for 355 yards and 6 touchdowns in an upset of the powerful Chicago Cardinals. Appropriately, he did it on Sammy Baugh Day in Washington.

> *You don't want to sit out there in the cold and see a fourteen-to-six game.*
>
> *Sammy Baugh*

The NFL underwent a couple of major alterations in 1937. Football came to the nation's capital as the Redskins moved from Boston to Washington. And offensive game plans began an inexorable drift away from three-yards-and-a-cloud-of-dust, toward a more freewheeling style of play.

CHUCK BEDNARIK

Linebacker-Center
Philadelphia (1949-1962)

UNLIKELY LEGACY
Pro football's last two-way player, Chuck Bednarik also is remembered for this devastating hit on Frank Gifford in 1960.

Football fans nicknamed Chuck Bednarik "Concrete Charlie" because he sold concrete in the offseason. They just as easily could have been referring to his style of play.

Bednarik played linebacker, then center, for the Philadelphia Eagles. And for a nine-game stretch when it mattered most, as the Eagles marched to the 1960 NFL title, he went both ways. Filling in for injured teammates on defense, he played 58 of 60 minutes in the NFL

Championship Game. And it was Bednarik who made the game-saving tackle, pinning Green Bay fullback Jim Taylor at Philadelphia's 8-yard line as time expired. The Eagles won 17-13, handing Packers coach Vince Lombardi his only postseason loss.

Bednarik grew up in the steel country of Bethlehem, Pennsylvania. He flew 30 missions as a waist gunner in a B-24 bomber during World War II before earning All-America status as a center at the University of Pennsylvania.

Bednarik missed two games during his rookie season in 1949, then only one more over the next 14 years. He was a sure tackler, an able blocker, and, occasionally, a one-man wrecking crew. During that 1960 title drive, he clobbered Giants halfback Frank Gifford with such force that Gifford missed more than a year of action. New York fans accused Bednarik of dirty play, but his body-slamming tackles were simply a product of his all-out play.

BOBBY BELL

Linebacker
Kansas City (1963-1974)

Jim Tatum, head coach at the University of North Carolina, liked what he saw in Bobby Bell, a big quarterback from Cleveland High School in Shelby, North Carolina. Unfortunately, Tatum's squad was not yet integrated. So he called some friends at the University of Minnesota to rave about Bell.

"I understand he's going to either Notre Dame or Michigan State, and they're both on our schedule in a couple of years," he said. "I don't want any 220-pound quarterback playing against us."

Bell didn't play much quarterback after high school. He won the Outland Trophy as a defensive tackle at Minnesota, then played defensive end for the Chiefs. In his third season, Chiefs coach Hank Stram moved Bell to outside linebacker, and he was devastating. He played in nine AFL All-Star Games and AFC-NFC Pro Bowls, and was voted to the All-Time AFL Team in 1969.

"He could have played tight end, running back, or even wide receiver, as fast as he was," Kansas City defensive tackle Jerry Mays said. "He could also throw the ball a mile."

In addition, Bell snapped for kicks for most of his career. A physical marvel with broad shoulders and a 32-inch waist, he returned 6 of his 26 career interceptions for touchdowns.

"Bobby Lee Bell," said his teammate and roommate, Buck Buchanan, "is the greatest athlete who ever was."

RAYMOND BERRY

End
Baltimore (1955-1967)

After he finally stopped catching passes from Johnny Unitas in Baltimore, Raymond Berry made a film called *There's a Catch to It*. It was a celluloid primer on the art of pass receiving. In it, he fielded throws from numerous angles and analyzed each in minute detail.

Even in retirement, Berry couldn't stop perfecting his craft.

Berry was no superman. He was 6 feet 2 inches and 187 pounds, with only decent speed. His vision was poor, and one of his legs was shorter than the other. So he simply outworked everyone else.

"We had some people who, if they would have made one-tenth the effort of Berry, would be in the Hall of Fame," Unitas said. "Raymond was willing to put the time and effort into it."

Time? Berry had Unitas throw him "bad passes" at practice, until the quarterback complained it was hurting his accuracy. Berry then talked his wife into making the throws. Effort? He claims to have had 88 distinct moves to get past a defender, and that he honed each one of them at every practice.

Berry helped the Colts win the NFL title in 1958, catching 12 passes for 178 yards against the Giants in the championship game, including 3 receptions on the game-tying drive. Berry had 631 catches, an NFL record, when he retired.

> **"**
> *We had some people who, if they would have made one-tenth the effort of Berry, would be in the Hall of Fame.*
> **"**
>
> *Johnny Unitas*

FRED BILETNIKOFF
Wide Receiver
Oakland (1965-1978)

The Oakland Raiders of the 1960s and 1970s were known for their "vertical" passing game. First, it was Daryle Lamonica lobbing bombs to Warren Wells, then Ken Stabler going deep to Cliff Branch. Through it all there was one constant: Fred Biletnikoff, whose brilliance in the short passing game opened up things for his speedier teammates. He was an integral part of the Raiders' offense for 14 seasons.

"Every scouting report we had on Fred said he was outstanding in college," said Al Davis, the Raiders' owner. "But scouts questioned his speed and weren't sure he'd be outstanding in the pros. We felt, with our approach to total pass offense, that speed wasn't the only consideration—that we could tailor our offense to our players."

But even the Raiders, who drafted Biletnikoff in the second round in 1965, were in need of proof. He played on special teams until the seventh game of his rookie season. When he finally did see action as a flanker, he caught 7 passes for 118 yards against the Patriots. For the next 13-plus seasons, he annoyed defenses all over the AFL and NFL. Biletnikoff retired in 1978 with 589 receptions, then a club record.

His performance in playoff games was even more impressive. The Raiders' go-to guy in 19 postseason games, he set NFL records (since broken) for catches (70), yards (1,167), and touchdowns (10). He earned MVP honors in Super Bowl XI after setting up 3 touchdowns in Oakland's 32-14 victory over Minnesota.

He did it with precise routes, liberal amounts of stickum (a glue-like substance, since banned, that he applied to his hands, jersey, and pants), and terrific hand-eye coordination. In one classic, back-and-forth game against Miami in the 1974 playoffs, Biletnikoff snared a sideline pass with one hand while a defensive back pinned his other hand to his side.

"The guy can catch anything he can touch," former Raiders coach John Madden said. "That's no accident. Some receivers might catch fifteen passes in practice. Fred will stick around and catch a hundred."

final NFL season. And he was strong enough to punish any receiver who managed to get open.

Still, Blount was a disappointment in his first two seasons. Miami's Paul Warfield burned him for 3 touchdowns in a 1971 game. After briefly considering retirement, Blount concluded that all he lacked was NFL-level knowledge.

"I had to realize every mistake I made was a lesson," he explained. "Instead of thinking about how many times I had been beaten, I decided to think about how many lessons I had learned."

Blount did not allow a touchdown pass in 1972. It was the "birth" of one of the game's best cornerbacks. He retired with 57 interceptions (still a Steelers' record), including an NFL-high 11 in 1975, when he was named league defensive player of the year.

Blount's exploits in the postseason included interceptions in Super Bowls IX and XIII, both of which came inside the Steelers' 20. His theft against Dallas in game XIII came with the score 14-14 late in the second quarter, and it led to a score that gave Pittsburgh the lead for good.

He so physically dominated receivers that when the league passed legislation limiting a defender's contact to a single bump in 1978, many referred to it as the "Blount Rule." But even that didn't curtail his effectiveness.

"A lot of cornerbacks want to be intimidating," Pittsburgh tackle Jon Kolb said. "They go through all kinds of things to be intimidating. Mel could walk out there, look down on the guy, and then run side-by-side with him. That was intimidating."

> " *I had to realize every mistake I made was a lesson. Instead of thinking about how many times I had been beaten, I decided to think about how many lessons I had learned.* "
>
> *Mel Blount*

MEL BLOUNT

Cornerback
Pittsburgh (1970-1983)

"When you create a cornerback," Steelers linebacker Jack Ham said, "the mold is Mel Blount. He was the most incredible athlete I have ever seen."

Blount had the perfect build (6-3, 205 pounds), and he was fast enough to run a 4.5-second 40-yard dash—in his fourteenth and

HALL OF STEEL
Mel Blount is one of eight Pittsburgh Steelers from the 1970s to be enshrined in the Pro Football Hall of Fame. He is joined by former teammates Terry Bradshaw, Joe Greene, Jack Ham, Franco Harris, Jack Lambert, and Mike Webster, as well as coach Chuck Noll.

TERRY BRADSHAW

Quarterback
Pittsburgh (1970-1983)

Looking back on his illustrious NFL tenure—four Super Bowl rings, back-to-back Super Bowl MVP awards, and a successful transition to FOX television studio analyst—it is easy to forget the frustration at the beginning of Terry Bradshaw's pro football career.

As the 1970 draft approached, the NFL flipped a coin to see which team, Pittsburgh or Chicago (each finished 1-13 in 1969), would get the first choice. The Steelers won, and to no one's surprise they took Bradshaw, a big-boned quarterback from Louisiana Tech.

A disastrous rookie season followed. Bradshaw passed for only 6 touchdowns, threw 24 interceptions, and was booed relentlessly at Three Rivers Stadium. His play improved after that and he even was on the passing end of Franco Harris's Immaculate Reception in the 1972 playoffs, but that didn't prevent him from spending the first six games of 1974, his fifth season, on the bench.

It wasn't until the middle of that season, when Steelers coach Chuck Noll made him the unqualified starter, that Bradshaw's career took off. Bradshaw made up for lost time, taking Pittsburgh to four Super Bowl titles in six years.

The Steelers' first two titles were led by a smothering defense. When that unit began to show its age, Bradshaw picked up the offensive pace. He passed for 318 yards and 4 touchdowns against Dallas to garner MVP honors in Super Bowl XII, which Pittsburgh won 35-31.

In game XIV, Bradshaw passed for 309 yards and 2 touchdowns, again winning MVP honors while directing Pittsburgh to a 31-19 victory over the Rams. His career average of 11.1 yards per attempt is a Super Bowl record.

Bradshaw's regular-season statistics included 27,989 passing yards and 212 touchdown passes. He also ran for 32 touchdowns.

"He's a special guy," said defensive tackle Joe Greene, teammate on all four championship teams. "He ran the gamut of emotions—in his private life and on the field…the successes, the failures. He overcame all of that. He has a story to tell."

JIM BROWN
Fullback
Cleveland Browns (1957-1965)

Critics who searched long and hard for some weakness in Jim Brown's play said he was not a good blocker—which is like saying Frank Sinatra wasn't much of a dancer. Brown was as pure a runner and as dominant a player as pro football has ever seen.

A phenomenal all-around athlete, he lettered in basketball and was an All-America lacrosse player at Syracuse. He finished fifth in the nation in the decathlon as a sophomore. The Cleveland Browns selected him with the sixth pick of the 1957 draft, and he soon became the yardstick for measuring NFL running backs.

Brown was among the fastest runners of his era. He also stood 6 feet 2 inches and weighed 232 pounds, big enough to cream a flat-footed linebacker. And durable? He carried the ball 2,359 times and never was forced to miss a down because of injury.

Someone once inquired of Paul Brown (no relation), Cleveland's wily coach, whether he might be overusing his fullback. "When you've got the biggest cannon," Paul Brown said, "you shoot it."

In nine seasons, Jim Brown led the NFL in rushing eight times. He fell short of 1,000 yards only twice, in his rookie year (when he had 942) and in 1962, when a sprained wrist limited him to 996. His most productive season was 1963, when he rushed for 1,863 yards on 291 carries (a 6.4-yard average) in 14 games.

For his career, he had 58 100-yard games (almost half of his total starts) and was selected to the Pro Bowl in each of his nine seasons.

Brown led Cleveland to the NFL title in 1964, and he was the league's most valuable player in 1965. But he walked away at the peak of his talents to become an action-adventure star, one of Hollywood's first African-American leading men. He left the game with 12,312 rushing yards and 126 touchdowns, records that survived for more than 20 years.

His record average of 5.2 yards per carry still is safe. So is his status as the NFL's most accomplished runner ever.

According to the Lions' Alex Karras, there was only one way to stop Brown: "Give each defensive guy on the line an axe."

ROOSEVELT BROWN

Tackle
New York Giants (1953-1965)

As much as anyone in NFL history, Roosevelt Brown proved that the cream eventually rises to the top.

His father didn't allow him to play football in high school because one of his uncles had been killed on the field. But Rosey's dad was a railroad man, away for long periods of time, and Brown played enough games to earn a scholarship to Morgan State.

A small, predominately black college in Maryland, it wasn't exactly Notre Dame. So the athletic lineman was virtually unknown as the 1953 draft approached. "We hadn't even heard of him," Giants owner Wellington Mara later said. "When we got through the first twenty rounds, we were just scraping the barrel."

In round 27, someone picked up a copy of the *Pittsburgh Courier* and spotted Brown—or, more accurately, spotted his measurements—on a Black College All-America team. The raw rookie won the Giants' starting left tackle spot in training camp, and he held it for 13 seasons.

At 6 feet 3 inches and 255 pounds, with a 29-inch waist, Brown was so fast that the Giants eventually rewrote their playbook, in essence making him a pulling tackle. He was named all-pro every year from 1956-1963, and he helped New York to the 1956 NFL championship.

WILLIE BROWN

Cornerback
Denver (1963-66)
Oakland (1967-1978)

Willie Brown wasn't just good at blanketing wide receivers. According to the former cornerback, he invented the technique.

"I was the first guy ever to bump-and-run," he said. "I had the size [6-1, 210] and speed and agility to cover somebody all the way down the field. The coaches didn't say anything about it because they'd never seen anybody do it."

Brown played tight end at Grambling, but he went undrafted in 1963. The Oilers tried to convert him to defensive back, but eventually cut him. The Broncos continued the experiment, and Brown became an all-AFL cornerback.

Brown cemented his reputation after a trade to Oakland in 1967. Employing a physical, in-your-face style, he became a nearly automatic Pro Bowl choice. And he never forgot how he got there. "I work at it," Brown once said. "Offseason, I'll go to the practice field, draw a line, set up five yards away, then imagine a guy running a post pattern on me."

Bowl center, and Buchanan wreaked havoc throughout the game. The Chiefs registered a surprisingly easy 23-7 victory.

Buchanan's effectiveness did not surprise the AFL linemen he had been tormenting for seven years. "He was such a dominant player," Stram said, "that they tried to double-team him when he came off the bus."

Buchanan was intelligent, durable (he did not miss a game in 13 seasons), and immense (6-7, 274). And he could move.

"I was big, but Buck was bigger," Oakland guard Gene Upshaw said. "You can't imagine that a guy that big can be so quick. I'd go at him, and it was like hitting a ghost."

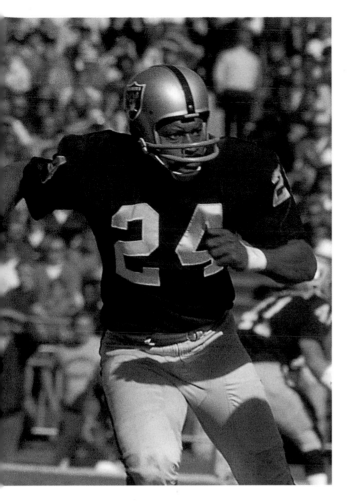

Brown sealed the Raiders' victory over Minnesota in Super Bowl XI by returning an interception 75 yards for a touchdown. Most of his 54 regular-season interceptions came early in his career. Toward the end, few quarterbacks were willing to challenge him.

BUCK ▶ BUCHANAN
Defensive Tackle
Kansas City (1963-1975)

The Minnesota Vikings were a powerful team in 1969, the final year before the AFL-NFL merger. They owned a 12-2 record and had averaged more than 27 points a game. They were heavily favored over the Chiefs in Super Bowl IV, but they were unprepared for one thing: Junious (Buck) Buchanan.

Kansas City coach Hank Stram lined him up directly over Mick Tingelhoff, the Vikings' Pro

DICK BUTKUS

Linebacker
Chicago (1965-1973)

Once, as the story goes, the Baltimore Colts were on their team bus, heading to the airport after a day of battle at Chicago's Wrigley Field. The bus stopped in heavy traffic and was jolted from behind. The Colts looked at one another and said, in unison, "Butkus."

Is it true? Does it matter? The feats that middle linebacker Dick Butkus performed on a football field have become so immense over the years, it is hard to discern fact from mythology.

Butkus was big (6-3, 245), but there were bigger defenders. He could move, but you wouldn't call him fast. What set him apart was unbridled ferocity, which he unleashed every time he took the field during a stellar nine-year career.

"With the highest respect," teammate Mike Ditka said, "I've got to say Dick is an animal. He works himself up to such a competitive pitch that on the day of the game he won't answer a direct question. He'll grunt."

Butkus's emotional fire took him a long way. He was so good at the University of Illinois that the trophy annually awarded to the nation's best collegiate linebacker bears his name. The Bears took him in the first round of the 1965 draft, along with another future Pro Football Hall of Fame player, running back Gale Sayers.

Butkus played in eight Pro Bowls in nine seasons. He enjoyed plenty of statistical success, including 25 opponents' fumbles recovered (the NFL record is 29) and 22 interceptions. But he suffered a knee injury in 1970, and the joint never fully healed. The knee had deteriorated so badly by the end of Butkus's career that trainers took to taping it in a bent position.

There was one further injustice dealt to Dick Butkus: Like Sayers, he never appeared in a playoff game.

"Football is something I was made for," Butkus said. "I guess my only regret is that my career was too short."

It wasn't for those who played against him. "If I had a choice, I'd sooner go one-on-one with a grizzly bear," Packers running back MacArthur Lane said. "I pray that I can get up every time Butkus hits me."

EARL CAMPBELL

Running Back
Houston (1978-1984)
New Orleans (1984-85)

Earl Campbell's career spanned nine seasons, but nagging injuries severely curtailed his playing time in two of them. Still, within that relatively narrow window of time, he may have been the most feared running back in the game.

Campbell was awesome to behold. He weighed 233 pounds, with 36-inch thighs and a barrel chest. Yet he could cover 40 yards in 4.6 seconds. When he broke loose, he often carried tacklers for yards or simply tossed them aside.

As Dallas safety Cliff Harris said, "All you can do is close your eyes and hope he doesn't break your helmet."

The Houston Oilers paid a steep price for "The Tyler Rose," who had won the 1977 Heisman Trophy at Texas. They traded three draft picks and Pro Bowl tight end Jimmie Giles to Tampa Bay for the first pick in the 1978 draft.

Houston wasn't complaining after the big back ran for 1,450 yards to become the first rookie to lead the NFL in rushing since Jim Brown in 1957. Campbell also led the league with 1,697 yards in 1979 and 1,934 in 1980, when he had four 200-yard games. He garnered NFL MVP notice all three seasons, including unanimous honors in 1979.

Bum Phillips, who had coached Campbell in Houston, brought him to the New Orleans Saints in a 1984 trade. By that time, Campbell had lost his burst. Still, considering the length of his career, his 9,407 rushing yards represent a monumental figure.

A Monday night game in his rookie year foretold his impact. He scored 4 times in a thrilling 35-30 victory over Miami, including an 81-yard fourth-quarter sprint when he simply was trying to convert a first down.

"That's the kind of thing that made him great," Phillips said. "When everybody else was getting worn down, Earl was still running."

> *When everybody else was getting worn down, Earl was still running.*
>
> *Bum Phillips*

one season. The next year, Csonka was the MVP of Super Bowl VIII after pounding the Vikings for 145 yards on 33 carries.

"My role is to make the power running game work," he said. "It's not a spectacular strategy, but I've lived and breathed it, and I know it works."

Csonka made headlines when he signed with the World Football League in 1975. That stint did little for Csonka's career, but he went on to play three years with the Giants, then returned to Miami for one season, earning NFL comeback player of the year honors for 1979.

▼WILLIE DAVIS

Defensive End
Cleveland (1958-59)
Green Bay (1960-1969)

In a 1960 trade that the Cleveland Browns would rather forget, they sent Willie Davis to Green Bay for an offensive end named A.D. Williams. Williams caught exactly 1 pass for the

▲LARRY CSONKA

Fullback
Miami (1968-1974, 1979)
N.Y. Giants (1976-78)

Coach Don Shula and fullback Larry Csonka, two tireless workers, enjoyed a tight bond during their years together in Miami. Csonka had played only a minor role during his first two seasons under coach George Wilson. When Shula took over, Csonka took center stage.

He tallied three consecutive 1,000-yard seasons from 1971-73, and they coincided with three Super Bowl appearances for the Dolphins, including victories in VII and VIII. In 1971, Csonka averaged 5.4 yards on 195 carries and had no fumbles.

In 1972, his bruising inside runs opened up the outside pitches for Eugene (Mercury) Morris, and the two became the first pair of 1,000-yard backs to play for the same team in

Browns. Davis became a five-time all-pro and played on five NFL championship teams.

Of course, he might never have attained such heights in Cleveland. Davis had played linebacker, guard, and tackle at Grambling, defensive end and offensive tackle for the Browns. The Browns planned to make him their starting left tackle before the trade.

Packers coach Vince Lombardi, ever one step ahead, told Davis he was a defensive end. Lombardi added that Davis's stay in Green Bay might be a short one if he couldn't adjust to the new position.

"I liked hearing that," Davis said, "because I thought my temperament was better suited for defense. Defense is really played with a certain frenzy, and my adrenalin flows pretty quickly."

At 6 feet 3 inches and 245 pounds, Davis was quick enough to flash by most of the league's blockers. He never missed a game in his career, and he recovered 21 opponents' fumbles, ranking second in NFL history when he retired. His postseason exploits included 3 sacks in Green Bay's 33-14 victory over the Raiders in Super Bowl II.

Davis proved equally formidable off the field. After earning a master's degree in business administration from the University of Chicago, he became a prominent entrepreneur in the Los Angeles area.

ERIC▶ DICKERSON

Running Back
Los Angeles Rams (1983-87)
Indianapolis (1987-1991)
Los Angeles Raiders (1992)
Atlanta (1993)

The NFL never had seen anything like Eric Dickerson when he joined the Los Angeles Rams in 1983. With his effortless, straight-up running style and the strange goggles he wore, he looked like a machine. But could he ever run.

Rams coach John Robinson was renowned for an overpowering ground game when he coached at Southern California, and Dickerson provided the legs Robinson needed to duplicate his system in the pros. Dickerson set NFL rookie records by running for 1,808 yards and scoring 18 touchdowns in 1983, then broke the NFL single-season record with 2,105 yards in 1984.

"He is the best I've seen, and I mean ever," said O.J. Simpson, the former record holder.

Dickerson gained 1,234 yards in 1985 and a league-leading 1,821 yards in 1986 before he was sent to Indianapolis as the focal point of a three-team trade in the 1987 season. The Rams acquired running back Greg Bell and a slew of draft picks, Buffalo received star linebacker Cornelius Bennett, and the Colts got a 1,000-yard rusher who helped lead them to their first playoff berth in 10 years.

Dickerson had his critics, who pointed to his fumbles and contract disputes. But there was no denying the facts. When the 6-3, 220-pound superstar retired after stints with the Raiders and Falcons, his 13,259 career rushing yards were second only to the great Walter Payton.

A CLASS OF HIS OWN
During the 1984 season, when Eric Dickerson set the NFL single-season rushing record at 2,105 yards, no other runner came within 400 yards of his effort, and the AFC leader, Earnest Jackson of San Diego, finished with 1,179.

MIKE DITKA

Tight End
Chicago (1961-66)
Philadelphia (1967-68)
Dallas (1969-72)

Most NFL historians agree that Green Bay's Ron Kramer was the first modern tight end, a sixth blocker who also ran pass routes. But Mike Ditka revolutionized the position.

Ditka was big enough (6-3, 225) and mean enough to block, and he had great hands. But it was his speed that turned defenses on their ears. He caught 56 passes for 1,076 yards (a 19.2-yard average) and 12 touchdowns in his first season, causing veteran Bears linebacker Bill George to say, "He is the best rookie I have ever seen."

Ditka played in five Pro Bowls in his first five seasons. In 1964, he caught 75 passes, a standard for tight ends that lasted 16 years.

The Bears won the NFL championship in 1963, and it's unlikely that they could have done it without Iron Mike. He broke six tackles to set up the game-tying field goal against Pittsburgh, threw a devastating block to spring Ronnie Bull for the only touchdown in a 10-3 victory over Baltimore, and caught a 22-yard touchdown pass against Detroit to clinch the Western Conference title.

Ditka signed with the AFL's Houston Oilers in 1966. But the AFL-NFL merger, announced shortly thereafter, voided all such contracts. Nonetheless, Bears owner George Halas traded Ditka to Philadelphia. Two years later, he went to the Cowboys.

Ditka never posted big receiving statistics after leaving Chicago, but he had no regrets. "Going to Dallas was like going to Heaven," he explained. "I had had all of the personal honors, and those were nice. But what I really wanted was a chance to go to the Super Bowl."

Opportunity knocked twice in Dallas. Ditka's Cowboys lost to Baltimore in Super Bowl V, but defeated Miami 24-3 in Super Bowl VI. Ditka scored the final touchdown in that game on a 7-yard reception.

He became a coach after his playing days ended, leading the 1985 Bears to a 15-1 season and victory in Super Bowl XX. In 1988, he became the first tight end enshrined in the Pro Football Hall of Fame.

TONY DORSETT

Running Back
Dallas (1977-1987)
Denver (1988)

Rewards seemed to come so easily to Tony Dorsett that it was easy to forget what an intense competitor he was.

In a phenomenal college career at Pittsburgh, he set NCAA records for rushing yards in a season (1,948 in 1976, when he won the Heisman Trophy) and a career (6,082), and became the first collegian to gain 1,000 yards in all four years of eligibility.

The Cowboys traded four picks to Seattle for the right to draft him with the second choice in 1977, but coach Tom Landry tried to bring him along slowly. Dorsett had other ideas, and despite starting only four games, he rushed for 1,007 yards, won NFL rookie-of-the-year honors, and helped Dallas win Super Bowl XII.

Dorsett, blessed with lightning speed, ran for 1,000 or more yards in each of his first five seasons and eight of his first nine. The season in which he fell short—the strike-shortened 1982 campaign—was one of his best.

He led the NFC with 745 yards that year. Against Minnesota in the season's final game, Dorsett took a handoff in the shadow of his end zone and sprinted 99 yards for a record that never will be broken. At the time, he had only nine teammates on the field!

"What impressed me was his tenacity," Landry said. "You could contain him for three quarters, but he would keep after it and break a long one to beat you in the fourth quarter."

Despite his slight build (5-11, 184 pounds), Dorsett was surprisingly strong. He missed only three games during his first nine seasons in Dallas. He rushed for 100 or more yards 46 times, and the Cowboys won 42 of those games. He retired with 16,293 yards from scrimmage, second only to Walter Payton at the time.

That total included one season in Denver. Broncos coach Dan Reeves, a former Cowboys assistant, made it clear why he worked a trade for the aging runner: "He is one of those players who, no matter where he goes, brings his team up to a new level. Above everything else, Tony Dorsett is a winner."

JOHN ELWAY

Quarterback
Denver (1983-1998)

No one ever questioned John Elway's ability. A talented athlete who was drafted on two occasions by major league baseball teams, he was earmarked for stardom the moment he joined the Denver Broncos in 1983.

Elway had it all. His arm was so strong that teammates talked about the Elway Cross, a mark that appeared on receivers' chests when they let his passes get past their hands. Cornerback Wymon Henderson once wandered in front of an Elway bullet at practice, and the ball lodged in his facemask. Elway was a gifted runner, too. He finished his career with more rushing attempts than any other quarterback in NFL history.

Elway was renowned for last-minute victories—he fashioned 47 game-winning or game-saving drives in the fourth quarter or overtime, including 5 in the postseason. But for a long time he seemed jinxed in Super Bowls. As the losses mounted—to the Giants in XXI, the Redskins in XXII, and the 49ers in XXIV—many began to wonder if the superstar quarterback would ever log a victory in the NFL's biggest game.

Elway's world changed in 1995 with the arrival of head coach Mike Shanahan and running back Terrell Davis. Shanahan, a former Broncos assistant, designed a well-rounded offensive scheme powered largely by Davis, and Elway flourished.

He put up big numbers, retiring second all-time in passing yards (51,475) and third in touchdown passes (300). When he led Denver to an exciting victory over Green Bay in Super Bowl XXXII, club owner Pat Bowlen held the Lombardi Trophy aloft and shouted, "This one's for John!"

But Elway saved his best for last. He not only had his best statistical season in 1998 (a 93.0 passer rating), he also became the first quarterback to start five Super Bowls. He bowed out with an MVP performance in Super Bowl XXXIII, passing for 336 yards to lead Denver to a 34-19 victory over Atlanta.

BRETT FAVRE

Quarterback
Atlanta Falcons (1991)
Green Bay (1992-present)

If you wanted to teach proper throwing mechanics, you would do well to compile a videotape of quarterback Brett Favre. Then package the tape as everything a quarterback is not supposed to do.

Favre, the Green Bay Packers' good ol' boy from Kiln, Mississippi (population: 50), tends to throw while moving away from the line of scrimmage. He often releases off his back foot, sometimes with a sidearm delivery. He gets away with flawed technique thanks to supreme confidence and tremendous arm strength.

"He makes throws that other quarterbacks wouldn't dare," says Mike Holmgren, Favre's coach in Green Bay for seven seasons. "He can throw with terrific velocity even when he is in quite awkward positions."

Favre is one of the most accomplished passers in NFL history. He is the only man to pass for 30 or more touchdowns in four consecutive seasons (1994-97), and the only three-time winner of the *Associated Press* NFL most valuable player award (1995-97, sharing the designation with Detroit's Barry Sanders the third time). Favre even put the title back in Titletown USA, leading the Packers over New England in Super Bowl XXXI.

By the end of the 1999 season, he had amassed some impressive statistics, including more than 30,000 passing yards and 235 scoring passes. But only one measure of individual worth truly stoked Favre's pride—his 125 consecutive regular-season starts, a modern-day record for durability at the position.

That feat surprised no one. When Favre was a senior at Southern Mississippi, he directed an upset of Alabama five weeks after suffering a cracked vertebra in an automobile accident.

SHINING STARR
When Brett Favre set the Packers' all-time records for pass completions, touchdowns, and yards, he surpassed standards set by Bart Starr (above), a legendary figure in Green Bay lore.

TOM FEARS

End
Los Angeles (1948-1956)

"
He was as fine a third-down receiver as anyone in the league.
"

Elroy Hirsch

A number of wonderful receivers have graced NFL fields in the last half-century. But none of them—not Raymond Berry or Jerry Rice, not Lance Alworth or Randy Moss—ever made as many receptions (18) in a single game as Tom Fears did against the Green Bay Packers on December 3, 1950.

It was no fluke. During his nine years in the NFL, Fears was as reliable a receiver as ever played. He set an NFL record with 77 catches in 1949, a mark that lasted one season—until he caught 84 in 1950. That record, set in a 12-game season (an average of 7 receptions per contest), would last more than a decade.

Later that year, when the Rams and Bears met in a playoff game with the National Conference crown and a berth in the NFL title game on the line, Fears was the difference. He scored on pass plays of 43, 68, and 27 yards in a 24-14 victory.

"He was as fine a third-down receiver as anyone in the league," Elroy (Crazylegs) Hirsch said. "He loved third-and-ten."

Fears and Hirsch were part of a virtually unstoppable Rams offense. Guided by the quarterback tandem of Bob Waterfield and Norm Van Brocklin and also featuring the punishing "Bull Elephant" backfield, they exhausted defenses all over the league.

They also won a title, with Fears playing a starring role. In the 1951 NFL Championship Game, the Rams and Cleveland Browns were tied 17-17 midway through the fourth quarter when Fears slipped between defenders Cliff Lewis and Tom James, caught Van Brocklin's pass at midfield as the defenders collided, and raced untouched to the end zone for the 73-yard touchdown that decided the game.

Fears, a lifelong Californian who played at Santa Clara and UCLA, began his NFL career as a defensive back. After he intercepted 2 passes and returned 1 for a touchdown in his first game, Rams coach Clark Shaughnessy had seen enough. He quickly moved Fears to offense, a decision that helped him earn a spot in the Pro Football Hall of Fame.

When Fears retired in 1956, he owned club records for most receptions in a game, season, postseason, and career.

OTTO GRAHAM

Quarterback
Cleveland (AAFC 1946-1949)
Cleveland (NFL 1950-55)

"The test of a quarterback is where his team finishes," legendary Cleveland coach Paul Brown once said. "By that standard, Otto was the best of them all."

He was talking about Otto Graham, and many historians agree with the assessment. Graham played 10 seasons as a pro and took the Browns to 10 championship games (four in the All-America Football Conference, six after they joined the NFL), winning 7 times. Graham was something of an unlikely candidate to become Paul Brown's field general. The son of two music instructors, he planned to concentrate on the French horn and basketball at Northwestern University. The football coach there spotted Graham participating in an intramural game and invited him to try out for the varsity team.

Pro football presented a much bigger challenge because Brown wanted to run the T-formation, a relatively complicated offense with which Graham had no experience. It didn't matter. Smart and instinctive, he conducted it like an orchestra.

Graham was a shifty runner and one of the most accurate passers of his day. ("A coach would tell me where to throw the ball, and I'd do it," he explained. "It was a God-given talent.") More than that, Graham was a charismatic leader. Though the Browns had tied for the NFL's best record in 1950, many still expected the AAFC refugees to fold against the Rams in the championship game. Instead, Graham passed for 4 touchdowns in a stunning 30-28 victory.

He was at it again in the 1954 NFL Championship Game, passing for 3 touchdowns and running for 3 more in a 56-10 rout of Detroit. That game was supposed to be Graham's last hurrah, but Brown talked him out of retirement for one final season. It ended with another title, capped with a 38-14 drubbing of Los Angeles in which Graham passed for 2 touchdowns and ran for 2 more.

In the late 1940s and early 1950s, titles were expected in Cleveland. They were Otto-matic.

AAFC LEGACY
The Browns were one of three teams to join the NFL in 1950 after the seven-team AAFC folded. The others were the 49ers and the Colts.

Chicago Bears embarked on a barnstorming tour in late 1925 and early 1926 that attracted huge crowds. Grange is credited with saving the sport in New York, and possibly everywhere else, for that matter.

Playing off Grange's drawing power, his agent, C.C. (Cash and Carry) Pyle, organized a rival league. Grange jumped to a new team in the new league—the New York Yankees of the AFL—in 1926, then returned to the NFL when the younger league folded.

A knee injury forced him to sit out the 1928 season. Although Grange returned to play six seasons with the Bears, he never regained his full agility. He did, however, find other ways to help his team.

For example, Grange's touchdown catch in a 1932 playoff game propelled the Bears to the NFL title. He also developed into a first-rate defensive back. He even made a game-saving tackle in the 1933 NFL Championship Game.

DARRELL ▶ GREEN
Cornerback
Washington (1983-present)

In his prime, Darrell Green was known as the perennial winner of the NFL's Fastest Man contest. As Green's career progressed, the focus became more significant: his status as one of the best cornerbacks in history.

The kid from Texas A&I made an immediate impact in Washington, starting as a rookie and returning an interception 72 yards for a score against the Rams in a 1983 playoff game.

That was just the first of his postseason heroics. Against the Bears in 1987, he returned a punt 52 yards for the winning touchdown, ignoring a tear to a rib-cage muscle suffered en route. The next week in the NFC title game, he broke up a fourth-down pass at the goal line to preserve a victory over Minnesota and allow the Redskins to advance to Super Bowl XXII, where he earned the first of two Super Bowl rings.

Green refused to slow down. In 1997, at 37, he became the oldest player ever to return an interception for a touchdown. Two years later, he became the oldest player to start at cornerback on opening day. He finished the 1999 season with 50 career interceptions and 250

▲ RED GRANGE
Halfback
Chicago Bears (1925, 1929-1934)
New York Yankees (AFL, 1926; NFL, 1927)

In an era in which college football reigned supreme, Harold (Red) Grange was king. Crowds flocked to see the carrot-topped "Galloping Ghost" from Illinois, a rare combination of speed, power, and flair.

"Grange runs as Nurmi runs and Dempsey moves, as a shadow flits and drifts and darts," wrote the famed Grantland Rice.

Grange turned pro the day after his final game at Illinois in 1925, bringing thousands of much-needed fans to the NFL. He and the

games played, both Redskins club records.

"Darrell's a walking encyclopedia on how to play corner," Washington defensive backs coach Tom Hayes said. "He's a fabulous resource for our team, our secondary, and me."

JOE GREENE ▶

Defensive Tackle
Pittsburgh (1969-1981)

Chuck Noll was hired to coach the woeful Pittsburgh Steelers in 1969 on the day before the NFL draft. The next day, Noll's first major act was selecting Charles Edward (Mean Joe) Greene, a little-known defensive tackle from North Texas State.

His nickname was a reference to his college team, the Mean Green. And while he never

cared for the nickname, opponents—and teammates—could attest to its relevance.

During training camp in Greene's rookie year, veteran Steelers offensive linemen Ray Mansfield and Bruce Van Dyke welcomed Greene to the NFL with a wicked high/low block. "He grabbed Bruce by the neck and me by the shoulder pads, and tossed both of us away like rag dolls," Mansfield said. "And then it took him about a half-second to get to the quarterback."

That was symbolic of Greene's 13-year career. He was voted to 10 Pro Bowls and twice was named NFL defensive player of the year.

Greene never was better than in 1974, when he began lining up in the gap between center and guard. His quickness off the line decimated blocking schemes, right up through Super Bowl IX, when he had an interception and a fumble recovery as the Steelers won their first of four NFL titles.

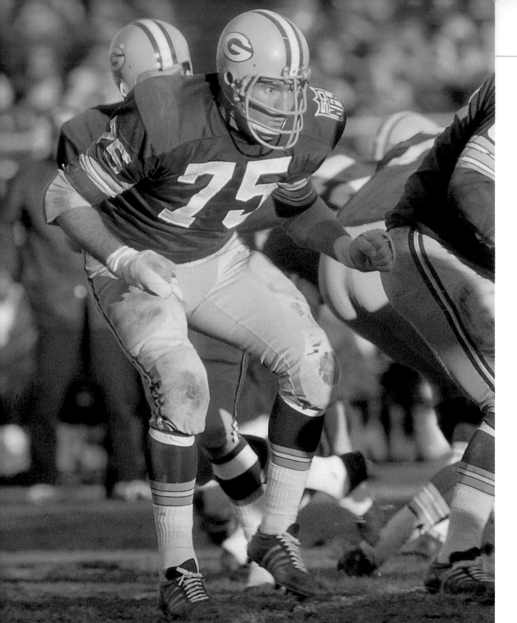

player. He played in 188 consecutive games from 1956-1971 (he missed the 1957 season because of military service), and he was voted to nine Pro Bowls. "He never blew up under pressure," Packers center Jim Ringo said. "He did everything with his head."

He had to. At a weight that fluctuated between 230 and 250 pounds, Gregg was smaller than most of his opponents. So he studied miles of film and relentlessly practiced his moves. "He had the best footwork I've ever seen on an offensive lineman," Redskins coach George Allen said. "They called him the best dancer since Fred Astaire."

Gregg's blocking helped pave the way for Green Bay's five NFL titles in the 1960s. He finished his career with one season in Dallas. Not surprisingly, the Cowboys won their first Super Bowl that year.

▼JACK HAM
Linebacker
Pittsburgh (1971-1982)

When most sports fans think of linebackers, they envision snarling wild men such as Dick Butkus or San Diego's Junior Seau. Jack Ham was cut from a different mold. He was

▲FORREST GREGG
Guard-Tackle
Green Bay (1956, 1958-1970)
Dallas (1971)

When guard Jerry Kramer was sidelined by an injury in 1965, Packers coach Vince Lombardi asked his best tackle, Forrest Gregg, to shift positions. Rather than diminish Gregg's chances for postseason honors, the change increased them. The *Associated Press* made him an all-pro guard; *UPI* honored him as a tackle.

"No matter where he plays," Lombardi said of Gregg, "he's the best man at the position."

On a team renowned for its steadiness, Gregg may have been the most dependable

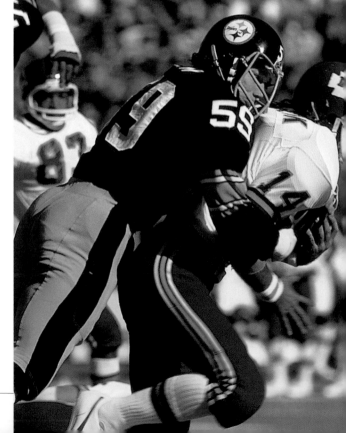

unassuming, cerebral, and multifaceted. He also was one of the best linebackers ever to chase a football.

Ham wasn't exactly built for stardom. A 185-pound high school senior, he barely managed to get Penn State's final scholarship. Even after he starred for two undefeated collegiate squads, NFL scouts doubted he was big enough (6-1, 225) for the NFL.

But Steelers coach Chuck Noll knew he had a player. Ham became a starter in the 1971 season opener, and he didn't relinquish his post until he retired 12 years later. Along the way he was selected to eight consecutive Pro Bowls (1973-1980 seasons) and three Super Bowls (he missed XIV with injuries).

Ham covered the field from sideline to sideline and was quick to sniff out running plays. But what set him apart was his pass coverage. He intercepted 32 passes in his career, and recovered 21 fumbles.

"Jack Ham remains the best outside linebacker I have ever seen," Noll said a few years ago. "Because he was a quiet kind of guy who didn't like attention, no one pushed him as the greatest thing ever. But he was a dominant player who basically had no weaknesses."

JOHN ▶ HANNAH
Guard
New England (1973-1985)

You could say that John Hannah was a genetically engineered offensive lineman. His father, Herb Hannah, played tackle for the Giants in the 1950s, and John's younger brother Charley played guard for the Buccaneers and Raiders in the 1970s and 1980s. But John owed his success to more than DNA. He labored until he became the NFL's premier guard.

"He was a tremendous competitor," said Ron Erhardt, who coached Hannah in New England. "There was never a time when he went through the motions."

Hannah (6-3, 285 pounds at his heaviest) never was the biggest guy on the field. His advantages were frightening strength and excellent speed. He was a familiar sight leading New England's sweeps, especially in 1978 when the team set an NFL record by rushing for 3,165 yards. He finished his career by playing in Super Bowl XX for the underdog Patriots.

Hannah was a starter for his entire career, missing only eight games because of injury. "To be great, you have to forget about pain," he said. "If it's not going to hurt you permanently, it's cheating your teammates if you don't play."

Hannah even lined up in 1984 and 1985, when he had to wear a brace to protect his chronically injured neck. As former linebacker Matt Millen said, "He had a high threshold for pain—both for himself and his opponent."

A PLAYER'S PLAYER
Of all the distinctions to come John Hannah's way, including nine Pro Bowl selections, no honor ranked higher than his designation as offensive lineman of the year four consecutive seasons (1978-1981), as determined by the NFL Players Association.

FRANCO ▶ HARRIS

Running Back
Pittsburgh (1972-1983)
Seattle (1984)

Before Franco Harris joined the Pittsburgh Steelers in 1972, the 40-year-old franchise never had won a postseason game. That changed when Harris led the Steelers into the AFC playoffs with 1,055 rushing yards, then stole a victory with his "Immaculate Reception."

"Franco was the guy who really lifted us to a new level," teammate Joe Greene said.

The Steelers won eight AFC Central titles and four Super Bowl rings during Harris's 12 years in Pittsburgh, but he remained an enigma. Nobody knew exactly how fast he was because he refused to go all out in time trials. He was a strong, 225-pound runner, but he often ran out of bounds in noncrucial situations. None of it mattered to "Franco's Army," his legion of followers in Pittsburgh.

Harris compiled eight 1,000-yard seasons and retired with a total of 12,120 rushing yards; at the time, he ranked third on the all-time list. But the numbers that mattered most were a record 354 rushing yards in the Super Bowl and 1,556 overall in the postseason, a mark that stood until the 1999 season.

"The thing that separated Franco was his ability to motivate himself for the big games," Steelers coach Chuck Noll said. "He got it done when the chips were on the line."

◀ MEL HEIN

Center
New York Giants (1931-1945)

Mel Hein may be the only NFL legend who owes it all—well, part of it, anyway—to the U.S. Postal Service.

Hein was a versatile lineman who led Washington State to the 1931 Rose Bowl. Hein wanted to play for the New York Giants, and the Giants expressed interest in him. By February of 1931, however, no offer had arrived from the Giants, so Hein signed a contract with the NFL's Providence Steam Roller and dropped it in the mail.

Lo and behold, a contract offer from the Giants—for more money—arrived the next day. Hein contacted the postmasters in Spokane, Washington, and Providence, Rhode Island. After pleading his case, he managed to reclaim his contract with the Steam Roller before it reached the club.

Hein went on to become a folk hero in New York. Long-time Giants owner Wellington Mara called him "the number-one player in the first fifty years of the Giants' history."

Hein's durability has attained mythic status. Even in his final season, at age 36, he routinely played 60 minutes a game. It is said he called time out only once—to re-set his broken nose.

Hein was a swift linebacker and a tireless center. He snapped the ball long to a Single-Wing tailback for most of his career. And he even caught shovel passes on trick plays. He was an eight-time all-NFL center (1933-1940), and the official league MVP in 1938. The fact that a lineman could win such an honor says something about football in the 1930s; it also says something about Mel Hein.

TED ▶
HENDRICKS

Linebacker
Baltimore (1969-1973)
Green Bay (1974)
Oakland-Los Angeles Raiders
(1975-1983)

There never was a player—or a personality—quite like Ted Hendricks.

He carried 235 pounds on a lanky 6-7 frame, and his long, muscular arms filled out a size-37 sleeve. It was this curious physical shape that engendered his nickname, "Mad Stork," when he played at the University of Miami.

Bill Curry, Hendricks's teammate when the two were with the Baltimore Colts, described him as looking "like a series of toothpicks with long, whippy, macaroni arms."

Hendricks's temperament was no less unusual. He once rode a horse onto the Raiders' practice field, wielding a traffic cone like a lance. Another time, he showed up wearing a helmet carved from a pumpkin. When rookie Howie Long took a breather for one play in 1981, Hendricks called time out and told his puzzled teammates, "I miss Howie."

But the measure of Hendricks's uniqueness was how well he played the game. He was an eight-time Pro Bowl choice, earning recognition at each of three different stops in his NFL odyssey. He also garnered four Super Bowl rings, one with Baltimore (V) and three with the Raiders (XI, XV, and XVIII).

"He had a kind of uncanniness about him," said Tom Flores, his long-time Raiders coach.

"He had a great feel for the game. He could almost anticipate the play before it happened."

Hendricks had 26 pass interceptions and recovered 16 fumbles in his career. His 4 safeties tied an NFL record, and his 25 blocked kicks are believed to be unprecedented.

Perhaps most remarkable, though, was his sheer durability, which many personnel experts had questioned when he arrived in the NFL. Hendricks closed out his career in 1983 with a 215-game playing streak.

A CURIOUS BIRD
Ted Hendricks was more than a football player. He was an honors graduate at the University of Miami whose hobby was "solving complex math problems." And he is the only member of the Pro Football Hall of Fame to be born in Guatemala.

ELROY ▶ (CRAZYLEGS) HIRSCH

Flanker
Chicago Rockets (AAFC 1946-48)
Los Angeles Rams (1949-1957)

When Elroy Hirsch was a halfback at Wisconsin, he had a good day against the Great Lakes Naval Station. Sportswriter Francis Powers, who had watched the game, wrote, "Hirsch ran like a demented duck. His crazy legs were gyrating in six different directions all at the same time."

From that day on, Hirsch would be known to the sporting world as Crazylegs.

From Wisconsin he transferred to Michigan (under the Navy's V-12 officer training program), then to the Marines' El Toro Air Station south of Los Angeles. His legend grew at each stage. He was expected to star for the Chicago Rockets of the All-America Football Conference, but injuries limited Hirsch's playing time.

By 1950, he was playing for the NFL's Rams, and coach Joe Stydahar shifted him to flanker. Hirsch took to receiving like a duck to water. In fact, he became one of the pioneers of the over-the-shoulder catch. He finished his pro career with 387 receptions for 7,029 yards.

"I can't remember Hirsch ever dropping a ball he could get his hands on," said Red Hickey, another of his mentors.

As the Rams powered to the NFL title in 1951, Hirsch was unstoppable. He won the receiving triple crown by leading the league with 66 receptions for 1,495 yards and 17 touchdowns in 12 games. Five of his scores came on plays of 70 yards or longer.

◀ PAUL HORNUNG

Halfback
Green Bay (1957-1962, 1964-66)

They called Paul Hornung the "Golden Boy." He had movie-star looks and a playboy's lifestyle. He lived life as he wished, which was one reason he sat out the 1963 season when Commissioner Pete Rozelle suspended him for

betting on NFL games. It added up to a less-than-serious image. But anyone who played against Hornung knew the intensity he brought to the field.

In 1956, Hornung became the first player from a losing team to win the Heisman Trophy. His Notre Dame squad finished 2-8. All he had to do to overcome such a hurdle was lead the Irish in passing, rushing, punt returns, kickoff returns, punting, and scoring. He finished second in tackles and interceptions.

Green Bay drafted Hornung first in 1957, but he had little impact until Vince Lombardi arrived in 1959. Then he was transformed.

In 1960, Hornung scored 176 points (15 touchdowns, 15 field goals, 41 extra points) in only 12 games, a league record that never has been seriously challenged. That year and the next, he was the NFL's most valuable player. While on special leave from the Army (he had been called up during the 1961 Berlin crisis), Hornung scored 19 points against the Giants in the 1961 NFL Championship Game, tying a record that would last 32 years.

As Packers guard Jerry Kramer said of Hornung, "He was the only player we had in Green Bay who came in a superstar and left a superstar."

SAM HUFF ▶

Linebacker
New York Giants (1956-1963)
Washington (1964-67, 1969)

The New York Giants knew Sam Huff was a football player when they drafted him in 1956. They just didn't know where they wanted to play him.

"He was an in-betweener," said Wellington Mara, the Giants' long-time owner. "He wasn't really big enough to be a defensive tackle, and he didn't seem quick enough to be a linebacker. The way we scout today, the computer would have spit him right out."

Fortunately for Huff, he did not have to return to the coal country of West Virginia, where he grew up. Giants assistant Tom Landry, tinkering with a scheme that would become the modern 4-3 defense, was looking for an alert, aggressive tackler to be his middle linebacker. He found one in Huff.

Huff played on six division winners and one NFL champion during his eight years in New York. His ground wars with fullbacks Jim Brown and Jim Taylor were the stuff of legends, but Huff's pass-defending skills were such that he also had 30 career interceptions. He played four subsequent seasons with Washington, then retired, only to come back for one final year as a player-coach under Vince Lombardi.

CBS once featured him in a made-for-TV documentary called *The Violent World of Sam Huff*. As any good middle linebacker would have been, Huff was flattered. "I wanted to rattle a guy's teeth," he said. "You hit him in the stomach or the ribs, and you hear uuurrrff. That's what I wanted."

SPOTLIGHT ON DEFENSE
The Violent World of Sam Huff not only captivated television audiences. It also created a new awareness of defensive stars in the NFL. "When I first came into the league," Sam Huff said, "they didn't even introduce defensive players at the start of the game."

AERIALISTS
The Green Bay passing attack of the 1930s and 1940s struck fear into opponents, ranking either first or second in passing yardage nine times in a 10-year span, from 1934-1943. Three of the reasons were (below) Don Hutson, Cecil Isbell, and coach Curly Lambeau.

DON HUTSON
End
Green Bay (1935-1945)

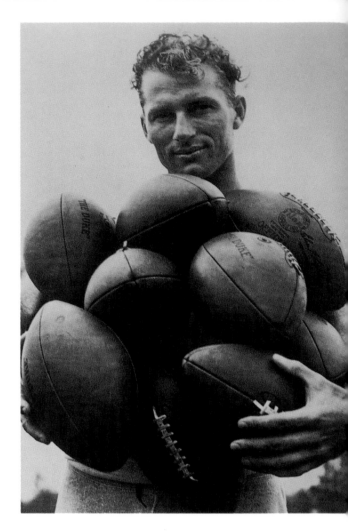

Most athletes have role models, but Don Hutson was on his own. Quite simply, no one who came before him could compare to the Alabama Antelope.

When Hutson joined the Packers in 1935, passing was something NFL teams did out of desperation, or as a form of trickery. He almost single-handedly changed that. Catching passes from Arnie Herber, then Cecil Isbell, he opened people's eyes to the possibility of the air attack. Hutson, who ran 100 yards in 9.7 seconds, had moves to complement his speed. One of his favorite moves involved grabbing a goal post (then positioned on the goal line) and quickly spinning himself to shake a defender.

"I just concede him two touchdowns a game and hope we can score more," Bears owner George Halas said.

Even that was easier said than done. Hutson helped the Packers win three NFL titles. In addition to his receiving, he was a superb defensive back (he intercepted 23 passes in his last four seasons), and a solid kicker.

But mostly he caught passes. During his glorious 11-year career, Hutson led the league in receptions eight times, in receiving yardage seven times, and in receiving touchdowns nine times. His 99 touchdown receptions established a career record that stood for 44 years. He won the NFL's most valuable player award twice and garnered All-NFL honors seven times.

His 1942 season ranks as one of the greatest ever. He caught 74 passes for 1,211 yards and 17 touchdowns in an 11-game schedule, and he scored 138 points to become the first NFL player to surpass 100. Hutson had 47 more receptions than any other receiver in the league that year, a mark that will likely never be surpassed. In 1944, he scored 29 points on 4 touchdowns and 5 conversions—in a single quarter.

"Nobody else in the league could touch him," Washington quarterback Sammy Baugh said. "You couldn't turn him loose on one man. He could hurt you pretty quick."

So opponents usually double-teamed Hutson, previously an unthinkable tactic. If that strategy is considered commonplace today, the modern-day receiver has Don Hutson to blame.

DEACON JONES

Defensive End
Los Angeles Rams (1961-1971)
San Diego (1972-73)
Washington (1974)

As a rookie in 1961, David Jones immediately announced that he preferred to be referred to as "Deacon."

"No one would remember a player called David Jones," he reasoned. "There are a thousand David Joneses in the phone book."

Creativity was one thing Deacon Jones always had in good supply. He coined the term "sack," because it connoted the devastation of an enemy city—and because it fit snugly in a headline. He also refined the head slap, a pain-inflicting move that later was outlawed. "You hadn't lived until you had your bell rung by Deacon a few times," Hall of Fame tackle Ron Mix said.

Still, the fourteenth-round draft choice was a long shot when he joined the Rams, having attracted scant attention at South Carolina State or Mississippi Vocational College. Even the Rams might have missed Jones had two of their scouts not traveled to Mississippi Vocational to check out a defensive back.

"Suddenly we saw this huge guy catch a tackle-eligible pass and outrun the defensive back," said Johnny Sanders, one of the scouts. "Well, we immediately rejected the defensive back and started a file on the tackle."

That was Jones, a raw talent whom the Rams converted to defense. For 11 years he manned the left side of Los Angeles's line, mostly next to tackle Merlin Olsen. They were the heart of the famed "Fearsome Foursome." Fearsome they were, especially Jones. In 1967, the Rams credited him with 26 sacks (then an unofficial statistic). That same year, the Rams surrendered only 25 sacks as a team.

Of course, being his teammate had its downside, too.

"It's really quite frustrating," Olsen once said. "You'll have a good shot at the ball carrier when—whap—Jones is sitting on him. I doubt if there ever has been a quicker big man in all of professional sports."

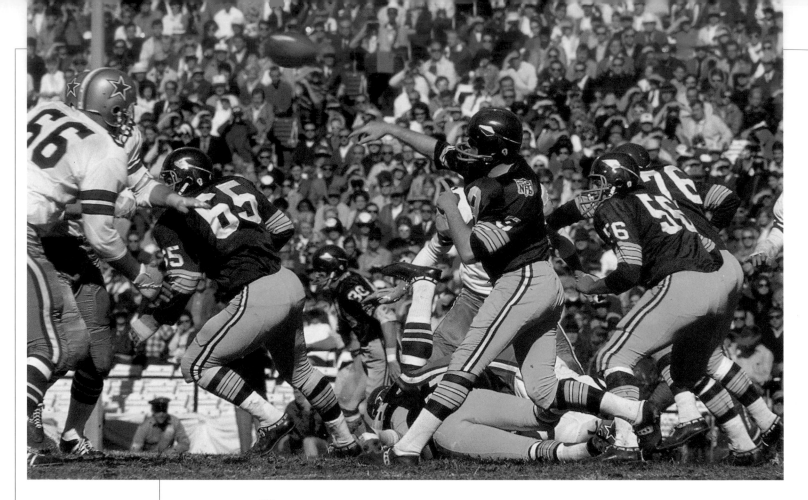

▲SONNY JURGENSEN

Quarterback
Philadelphia (1957-1963)
Washington (1964-1974)

Sonny Jurgensen's passes were so pretty and his ability to unload the ball under pressure was so uncanny that he won fans all over the nation. Some of them were fellow quarterbacks.

"If I threw as much as Jurgensen, my arm would fall off," Johnny Unitas said. "And if I could throw as well, my head would swell up too big to get into a helmet."

Jurgensen's arm never fell off, but he did undergo nine surgeries during his 18-year career. That was the result of playing for a long line of mediocre teams.

Jurgensen backed up Norm Van Brocklin when the Eagles won the NFL title in 1960. A year later, as the starter, he set NFL records for completions, yards, and touchdown passes. Six years later, after a trade to Washington, he upped the marks for completions and yards, and also set a league record for attempts. He led the NFL in passing yards five times.

Through it all, he never looked the part. Carrying 203 pounds on a 6-foot frame, he looked almost unathletic. One of his Redskins teammates said he had a body better suited for pro bowling than pro football.

"The way I looked was one of the appeals I had to the fans," he said. "Joe Six-Pack could...look at me and say to his wife or his buddy, 'See, that guy's got a stomach, too, and he can play.'"

PAUL KRAUSE ▶

Safety
Washington (1964-67)
Minnesota (1968-1979)

In the case of Paul Krause, baseball's loss was the NFL's gain.

Krause was a superb center fielder for the University of Iowa who once threw out four runners at the plate in a single game. But he injured his right shoulder in a football game as a junior, effectively ending his baseball career.

Even on the football field, Krause played like a center fielder. He intercepted 2 passes against Cleveland in his first NFL game. He went on to collect a league-high 12 interceptions for Washington in 1964, and by the end of his career he had amassed an NFL-record 81.

Most of those takeaways came in a Vikings' uniform. In 1968, Minnesota coach Bud Grant had the "Purple People Eaters" up front to harass opposing quarterbacks. What he needed, he said, was "an intelligent, far-ranging free safety with great hands."

Grant traded for Krause, who became an eight-time Pro Bowl pick (six with the Vikings), a four-time Super Bowl starter, and a genuine ball hawk.

Grant explained: "He was, in a sense, free to play down and distance, the tendencies, the quarterback's eyes, double the key receivers, play a hunch, use his intelligence and athletic ability to be the greatest free safety of all time."

mean streak that was just about as wide as the Ohio River.

"Jack lived to play," Steelers defensive tackle Joe Greene said. "He had a great attitude. I loved it. He didn't like you if you had on a different-color jersey. Heck, he didn't like half the guys with the same jersey on."

When the Steelers drafted Lambert in the second round in 1974, they discovered the final piece of the Steel Curtain defense. Lambert started immediately (he even drove to Pittsburgh every weekend that spring and summer before his first training camp to meet with linebackers coach Woody Widenhofer) and held the job for 11 seasons. He played in nine straight Pro Bowls (1975-1983 seasons) and was named NFL defensive player of the year in 1976.

Most fans, thinking of Lambert's toothless scowl and relentless fury, remember him as a classic run-stuffer. He was that, to be sure, but he also intercepted 28 passes during his career.

"Of all the great middle linebackers," said teammate Jack Ham, "what set him apart was his ability to play the pass. He was the best, most complete middle linebacker to ever play the game."

JACK ▶ LAMBERT

Linebacker
Pittsburgh (1974-1984)

Jack Lambert did something no human should be able to do. He played middle linebacker in the NFL at 220 pounds. To manage this unlikely feat, he relied on quickness, anticipation, and a

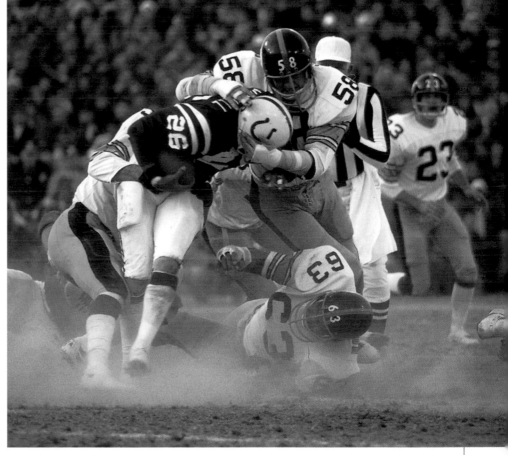

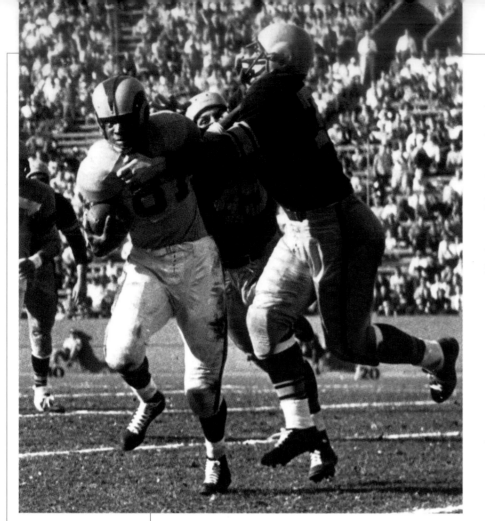

the NFL's most enduring records. After later stints with the Chicago Cardinals and Detroit Lions, he retired with 68 interceptions.

In an era of little finesse, Lane was an ideal fit. He covered his men one-on-one, never afraid to supply a little pounding. Lane was known for his high, hard tackles.

"He gambles," Lions receiver Jim Gibbons said, "but he recovers if it's going wrong. That's what separates him from most corner men—his natural reflexes. There's no one like him."

WILLIE ▼ LANIER
Linebacker
Kansas City (1967-1977)

Willie Lanier dished out a fair amount of punishment during his stellar 11-year career with the Chiefs, and he absorbed more than a little himself. Lanier suffered so many concussions that he started wearing a special

MUSIC MAN
Dick (Night Train) Lane acquired his nickname during training camp in his rookie year when a teammate, Ben Sheets, spotted him in the same room where the popular song "Night Train" was blaring on a record player.

MUSIC MAN
Dick (Night Train) Lane acquired his nickname during training camp in his rookie year when a teammate, Ben Sheets, spotted him in the same room where the popular song "Night Train" was blaring on a record player.

A RECEIVER, TOO
Night Train Lane earned his place in the Pro Football Hall of Fame with his sterling play on defense. But he also owns a spot in the Cardinals' record book as a receiver. On November 13, 1955, he caught a 98-yard pass against Green Bay, equaling a club record that stands today.

▲ NIGHT TRAIN LANE
Cornerback
Los Angeles Rams (1952-53)
Chicago Cardinals (1954-59)
Detroit Lions (1960-65)

Sometimes it pays to have chutzpah. Dick (Night Train) Lane just had quit a job in an aircraft factory when, while riding a bus down Beverly Boulevard in Los Angeles, he spotted the Rams' office. He returned, armed with a scrapbook of his modest football exploits—at Scottsbluff Junior College in Nebraska and at Fort Ord Army base in California—and asked to see the head coach.

This was 1952, long before the rise of NFL scouting departments. Lane not only got his meeting, he was invited to training camp. His break came when the Rams' defensive backfield became depleted and coach Joe Stydahar moved Lane from offensive end to cornerback.

Lane learned enough to intercept 14 passes (in 12 games) during his rookie season, one of

helmet fitted with a foam "bumper." If it helped Kansas City win football games, so be it.

Lanier was a pioneer, the first black player to line up at the high-profile middle linebacker position. In addition to his size (6-1, 245), he brought speed, strength, and emotion to the position, earning berths in two AFL All-Star Games and the first six AFC-NFC Pro Bowls.

"You hear a lot about Dick Butkus and Tommy Nobis," Dallas assistant coach Ermal Allen said. "But Willie Lanier is really the best middle linebacker in pro football."

Lanier moved into the starting lineup four games into his rookie season. On one side of him was Bobby Bell, on the other Jim Lynch. Until Bell's retirement in 1974, they formed one of the NFL's most daunting defensive trios. In 1969, the Chiefs' defense led the way to a Super Bowl title, holding three postseason opponents to a total of 20 points (including a 23-7 victory over Minnesota in Super Bowl IV).

Lanier never was better than in his lone Super Bowl appearance. In one three-play stretch at the outset of the fourth quarter, he stopped successive running plays by Dave Osborn and Oscar Reed, then intercepted a pass intended for John Beasley.

Lanier usually was at the point of attack. He recorded 27 career interceptions, recovered 15 fumbles, and made enough tackles to earn a vivid nickname: "Contact."

STEVE ▶ LARGENT

Wide Receiver
Seattle (1976-1989)

In 1994, Steve Largent was elected to the U.S. House of Representatives from Oklahoma's First Congressional District. No one should have been surprised. Steve Largent rarely failed at anything he set his mind to.

Largent topped the nation in touchdown receptions as both a junior and a senior at the University of Tulsa, but because of his modest frame (5-11, 187) and average speed, he was only a fourth-round draft choice of the Houston Oilers—and they were ready to cut him late in the preseason. His savior was Jerry Rhome, who had coached Largent at Tulsa and, in 1976, was an assistant with the expansion Seahawks.

Seattle got Largent for an eighth-round pick.

He caught 54 passes as a rookie. The next year he began a streak of 177 games with at least 1 catch. A season after that, he led the AFC with 71 receptions, and in 1979, he led the NFL with 1,237 receiving yards.

By the time he decided to retire after the 1989 season, Largent had established NFL standards for catches (819), yards (13,089), and touchdowns (100).

"He was such a smart player," opposing safety Mike Reinfeldt said. "With all his moves and outs and ups, he used to drive cornerbacks crazy. He had quickness and talent that did not always show up on a stopwatch or a measuring stick."

TOO SLOW, TOO SHORT
When Steve Largent arrived in the NFL, some talent scouts questioned whether he had the size or the speed to make it in the pro game. Many years later, Hall of Fame cornerback Mike Haynes made light of the doubters. "For a guy too slow and too short," he told Largent, "you sure fooled a lot of people."

BOBBY LAYNE

Quarterback
Chicago Bears (1948)
New York Bulldogs (1949)
Detroit (1950-58)
Pittsburgh (1958-1962)

Detroit Lions halfback Doak Walker uttered the line that best summarized quarterback Bobby Layne's career. "Bobby Layne never lost a game in his life," Walker said. "Time just ran out on him."

Layne was not the most accurate passer in the game. He completed fewer than 50 percent of his attempts. But he was the kind of leader, who, with a game on the line, had few peers. "He is the best third-down quarterback in the game," Browns coach Paul Brown said.

Brown knew as well as anyone. Layne beat his Cleveland teams in consecutive NFL Championship Games in 1952 and 1953. In the 1953 game, the Lions took possession at their 20-yard line, trailing 16-10 with 4 minutes 10 seconds to play. Layne promptly completed 4 of 6 passes for 77 yards, capped by a 33-yard touchdown strike to end Jim Doran that gave Detroit a 17-16 victory.

When the Lions played for the title again in 1954, they were smothered 56-10 by the Browns. Layne claimed he performed poorly in the game because he had gotten too much sleep the night before—that is, more than his requisite five hours.

As good as Layne was with a football, he was just as formidable with a beer mug. He was the life of every party and he was revered by his teammates. But Layne's good-ol'-boy persona masked a red-hot competitiveness and some remarkable all-around athletic skills. He won 26 consecutive games as a pitcher at the University of Texas, and he did double duty as his team's kicker for four NFL seasons. In that role, Layne scored 99 points in 1956 to lead the league.

The numbers that earned him immortality in the Pro Football Hall of Fame were 1,814 pass completions, 26,768 yards, and 196 touchdown passes (all records when he retired)—and, of course, two world championships.

Even in the twilight of his career, after he was traded to Pittsburgh in 1958, he elevated the hapless Steelers to back-to-back winning seasons for the first time in franchise history.

BOB LILLY

Defensive Tackle
Dallas (1961-1974)

Bob Lilly, born and raised in Throckmorton, Texas, became the living incarnation of the Dallas Cowboys. The peerless defensive tackle was the franchise's first draft pick (1961), its first Pro Bowl choice (1962), the first member of its "Ring of Honor" (1975), and its first Pro Football Hall of Fame inductee (1980).

For a while, he also became the symbol of the club's tendency to fall short of glory. The Cowboys became known as "Next Year's Champions" after a series of heartbreaking playoff defeats in the late 1960s and early 1970s. The low point was a bumbling 16-13 loss to Baltimore in Super Bowl V. After Dallas lost on a last-second kick, Lilly got so frustrated he tossed his helmet 40 yards through the air.

A year later, he was a different sort of poster boy. This time, the Cowboys trounced the Dolphins 24-3 to become NFL champions. Lilly contributed a key play in that effort, chasing down quarterback Bob Griese for a 29-yard loss.

"I didn't think a man that big could be so quick," Miami guard Bob Kuechenberg said.

Lilly was at least that quick. The 6-foot 5-inch, 260-pound lineman also boasted exceptional upper-body strength, which allowed him to fight through constant double- and triple-team blocking. Lilly had exceptional field vision, and was so durable he never missed a regular-season game in 14 seasons.

He began his pro career as a defensive end and was good enough to make the Pro Bowl. But when coach Tom Landry moved Lilly inside, the "Doomsday Defense" had its cornerstone, and the Cowboys were on their way to eight consecutive playoff appearances.

"A man like this comes along once in a generation," said Landry. "There won't be another Bob Lilly in my time."

> **"**
> *A man like this comes along once in a generation. There won't be another Bob Lilly in my time.*
> **"**
>
> *Tom Landry*

RONNIE LOTT

Cornerback-Safety
San Francisco (1981-1990)
Los Angeles Raiders (1991-92)
New York Jets (1993-94)

Late in the 1985 season, the 49ers' doctors recommended surgery to repair the tip of Ronnie Lott's left pinky finger. But that would have meant missing the playoffs. Lott simply had them amputate above the third knuckle; he didn't miss a down.

"He doesn't care about his own body," quipped Randy Cross, his teammate in San Francisco for eight seasons, "so why should he care about yours?"

If you were trying to gain yards against his 49ers, all that Lott cared about was laying you flat. His boyhood hero was Dick Butkus, and he became a similar role model to a generation of would-be hitters.

"He's like a middle linebacker lined up at safety," Dallas coach Tom Landry said. "He's devastating. He may dominate the secondary better than anyone I've seen."

Lott wasn't simply a battering ram, of course. He was drafted as a cornerback, and he played his first four seasons at that position, earning Pro Bowl honors each year (then six as a safety). He started as a rookie and returned 3 of his 7 interceptions for touchdowns, helping the 49ers to victory in Super Bowl XVI. He earned three more rings before finishing his career with the Raiders and Jets.

Lott intercepted 63 passes in his career, plus an NFL-record-tying 9 in the postseason. His big hits were too numerous to count.

SID ► LUCKMAN

Quarterback
Chicago Bears (1939-1950)

After the Chicago Bears dispatched the Washington Redskins 73-0 in the 1940 NFL Championship Game—the biggest title-game blowout in the history of American team sports—nearly every team in the league installed the T-formation Chicago used in the game. However, no other team was able to mimic the Bears' success because none of them had Sid Luckman at quarterback.

Luckman was a classic Single-Wing back at Columbia, a nimble runner who attempted an occasional pass to keep defenses honest. He struggled mightily with the T for a short time, but soon became its most gifted practitioner.

Luckman had many great seasons in Chicago, but none to match 1943, when he was named league MVP after setting records for passing yards (2,194) and touchdowns (28). Against the Giants in November of that year, he became the first NFL quarterback to pass for 7 touchdowns in one game (on Sid Luckman Day at the Polo Grounds). He capped the season by again beating the Redskins in the championship game, this time firing 5 touchdown passes in a 41-21 triumph.

Luckman also took the Bears all the way in 1941 and 1946. The latter title came a few months after he had turned down $25,000 to become player-coach of the AAFC's Chicago Rockets. His reasoning: "How could I quit a club that had done so much for me?"

"He was such a powerful, explosive football player," Shula said, "both as a receiver and a blocker. He had great speed. After he caught the ball, he had great running ability. As a blocker, he would explode out of his stance and get into the linebacker's face, and just overwhelm him."

Speed was Mackey's trump card. Twice, in 1963 and 1965, he averaged more than 20 yards per catch. He had 9 touchdowns in 1966, 6 of them on plays of 50 yards or more. The most memorable of Mackey's receptions came in Super Bowl V, when he caught a twice-tipped pass from Johnny Unitas and rumbled for a 75-yard touchdown. The wild play gave Baltimore its first touchdown in a 16-13 victory.

MULTITASKER
Like other players of his era, Sid Luckman was a two-way player. Unlike most, however, he was exceptional at just about everything he did. As a quarterback, he had 137 touchdown passes. As a defensive back, he had 17 interceptions. As a punter he averaged 38.6 yards on 230 attempts.

JOHN ▶ MACKEY

Tight End
Baltimore (1963-1971)
San Diego (1972)

John Mackey wanted to be a lawyer when he was growing up on Long Island. He was accepted by Georgetown Law School after graduating from Syracuse with a history degree, but he decided to opt for an equally contentious line of work: professional football.

Mackey joined the Colts the same year as head coach Don Shula, and he quickly became a ground-breaking tight end. Many people consider Mike Ditka, one of Mackey's contemporaries, to be the first great tight end. But when an All-Time NFL Team was selected by Pro Football Hall of Fame panelists in 1969, it was Mackey who got the nod.

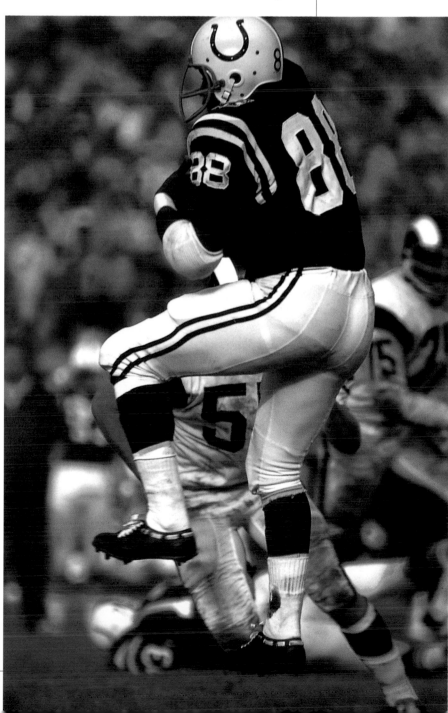

GINO MARCHETTI

Defensive End
Dallas (1952)
Baltimore (1953-1964, 1966)

Gino Marchetti's Italian-immigrant father was so shocked by the game of football that he couldn't bring himself to watch his son's games until Gino was established as an NFL star. Finally, in December of 1958, the elder Marchetti turned on his television to watch the Colts and Giants battle in the NFL Championship Game.

So what happened? Gino broke his leg in two places.

Though upsetting, the injury was a perfect symbol of Marchetti's career. For one thing, it occurred as he made a pivotal tackle of New York running back Frank Gifford. It also showed Marchetti's old-school toughness.

Refusing refuge in the locker room, he insisted on watching most of the remainder of the game from the sideline. Afterward, his teammates presented him with the game ball.

Only an injury of that magnitude could keep Marchetti away from the Pro Bowl. He made it every other year from the 1954 season through 1964. A can't-miss tackler and a fierce pass rusher, Marchetti was named the top defensive end of the NFL's first 50 years in 1969.

"He had the look of death in his eyes on the field," said Leo Nomellini, a defensive tackle of the same era. "There was no way to keep him off the passer or ball carrier. He knocked down blockers like they were rag dolls."

Marchetti's heroism was not relegated to the football field. The medals he won while fighting with the U.S. Army's Sixty-Ninth Infantry division in Europe during World War II helped win his parents their release from an American internment camp. On two occasions, the Colts talked Marchetti out of retirement. The second time was 1966, when, after more than a year off, he plugged a hole at defensive tackle and helped the team to a 9-5 record.

DAN MARINO

Quarterback
Miami (1983-1999)

When Dan Marino retired in March, 2000, fans lamented the fact that he never won a Super Bowl with the Dolphins. A close look at his career passing statistics suggests that his defensive opponents are the ones who should be pitied.

After setting records at the University of Pittsburgh (only four blocks from the house in which he grew up), Marino became part of the famed quarterback class of 1983. He was the sixth quarterback selected in the first round of the NFL draft, but he was the first to become a star as a professional.

Marino led the AFC in passing and made the Pro Bowl as a rookie in 1983, but it was a quiet prelude to his gaudy 1984 season. He did not just break records that year, he ground them into dust. Throwing largely to the Marks Brothers—wide receivers Mark Duper and Mark Clayton—he finished with 5,084 yards and 48 touchdown passes.

Marino continued to compile staggering numbers throughout his 17-year career, which was distinguished by nine selections to the Pro Bowl. He walked away with more than 20 NFL records, including career marks for most attempts (8,358), completions (4,967), passing yards (61,361), and touchdowns (420).

"Nobody likes to have their records broken," said Fran Tarkenton, the previous holder of all four marks, "but I'm very proud to have Danny break them. And I don't think that anybody will break those records in his lifetime."

Far from agile, Marino relied on uncanny field vision, guile, and one of the quickest releases known to man. "He sees it, it's gone," former teammate Jim Jensen said. "There's no thinking."

No performance provided better evidence than a game against the New York Jets in 1988, when Marino completed 35 of 60 passes for 521 yards and 3 touchdowns—in a defeat.

Despite the lack of a Super Bowl ring, Marino always was a winner. In 37 games, he transformed a fourth-quarter deficit into a Miami victory. As former quarterback Len Dawson explained, "He is one of those players who believes he's never out of it."

happy to watch Matson light up the field with his luminescent style.

Matson was big (6-2, 220) and fast. He ran the 100-yard dash in 9.5 seconds. Fresh from the 1952 Helsinki Olympics, where he won a bronze medal in the 400-meter run and a gold in the 1,600-meter relay, he was hailed as "The Messiah" by the Cardinals. He took them nowhere, but the Rams were impressed enough to trade *nine* players for Matson in 1959. He later played for Detroit and Philadelphia.

There was little Matson couldn't do with a football. He was a darting halfback, a solid receiver, an enthralling kick returner, and an underrated defensive back. He scored 40 touchdowns rushing, 23 on receptions, 9 on kick returns, and 1 on a fumble recovery. He led the NFL in punt-return average (18.8 yards) in 1954, and kickoff-return average (35.5) in 1958.

"The only problem he gave a coach was where to play him," reporter Bob Oates wrote.

HUGH ▶ McELHENNY

Halfback
San Francisco (1952-1960)
Minnesota (1961-62)
New York Giants (1963)
Detroit (1964)

> "
> *The only problem he gave a coach was where to play him.*
> "
>
> *Bob Oates*

▲ OLLIE MATSON

Halfback
Chicago Cardinals (1952, 1954-58)
Los Angeles (1959-1962)
Detroit (1963)
Philadelphia (1964-66)

No matter where he went, Ollie Matson played for struggling teams. During 14 NFL seasons, his teams finished with a winning record only twice. He never saw action in a postseason game. But to those who loved football, it made little difference. They were

Playing against Detroit in a 1957 playoff game, San Francisco's Hugh McElhenny caught a short pass and broke free for a 47-yard touchdown. When the 49ers subsequently reviewed the film, they figured that with his broken-field running he actually ran farther than 100 yards on the play. It was vintage McElhenny, who may have been the greatest open-field runner of all time.

McElhenny never led the league in rushing. But his instantaneous cuts, gravity-defying spins, and amazing changes of direction served to explain why he was nicknamed "The King."

McElhenny started quickly after joining the San Francisco 49ers in 1952. In his rookie year, he recorded the season's longest run (89 yards), its longest punt return (94), and its best rushing average (7.0 yards per carry). He also made the first of six Pro Bowl appearances.

have too much respect for you to quibble over a thousand dollars," Gillman told his star player.

"Coach," Mix replied, "I have too much respect for a thousand dollars not to quibble."

Through it all—eight AFL All-Star Games, five AFL Championship Games with the Chargers, and selection to the All-Time AFL Team in 1969—Mix never lost his wry sense of humor.

Eclectic and articulate, he was an unlikely candidate for the bruising world of pro football. Indeed, Mix preferred baseball and track in high school. But when he received a scholarship to play football at Southern California, he added nearly 100 pounds to his frame and became a force on the offensive line.

Mix never weighed more than 255 pounds, but he consistently dominated the league's defensive mammoths with an unequaled repertoire of textbook techniques. It is said that during his 10 years in the AFL, he was called for holding penalties on only two occasions. He rarely surrendered a sack, though Gillman's wide-open offense put the ball in the air at every opportunity.

"The Intellectual Assassin" made a lifetime of upending stereotypes. One of the few Jewish football stars, Mix opened a legal practice in San Diego after his football career.

"When Hugh joined the Forty-Niners in 1952," former general manager Lou Spadia said, "it was questionable whether our franchise could survive. McElhenny removed all doubts. That's why we call him our franchise saver."

He joined the expansion Vikings in 1961, and McElhenny had what he considered his finest season, compiling 1,097 all-purpose yards for the first-year squad. When he retired after the 1964 season, he was one of only three NFL players with more than 11,000 combined yards.

RON MIX ▶

Guard-Tackle
Los Angeles-San Diego (1960-69)
Oakland (1971)

Once, in the course of contract negotiations, Chargers tackle Ron Mix and head coach-general manager Sid Gillman found themselves separated by a gulf of $1,000 per year. "Ron, I

JOE MONTANA

Quarterback
San Francisco (1979-1992)
Kansas City (1993-94)

When Joe Montana arrived at the San Francisco 49ers' training camp as a rookie in 1979, wide receiver Dwight Clark mistook him for a free-agent kicker.

The pair later would team on one of the most famous pass plays in NFL history (against Dallas in the 1981 NFC Championship Game), but Clark's initial confusion can be forgiven. Montana looked like the pizza delivery guy— until he stepped into the huddle, where he turned into Superman.

Montana took the 49ers to four Super Bowl triumphs, and he did it with a variety of styles. The 1984 and 1988 editions were balanced with a strong running game. The 1989 team threw the ball without regard for situation. And the 1981 49ers? That title team remains something of a mystery, except that the 49ers had Montana coolly directing Bill Walsh's early model West Coast Offense.

Montana is the only three-time Super Bowl most valuable player. He attempted 122 passes without an interception in his four appearances in the Big Game.

If the wiry quarterback was consistently superb—his career passer rating of 92.3 ranks second all-time—he was positively uncanny in pressure-packed situations. In his last collegiate game, he led Notre Dame from a 22-point deficit to win the 1979 Cotton Bowl. And against Cincinnati in Super Bowl XXIII (his only appearance in which he was not named MVP), he calmly guided the 49ers 92 yards in the final minutes, firing the game-winning touchdown pass to John Taylor with 34 seconds left.

"When the game is on the line, and you need someone to go in there and win it right now," Walsh said, "I would rather have Joe Montana as my quarterback than anyone else who ever played the game."

In 1993, after injuries interrupted Montana's career, San Francisco dealt the legendary passer to Kansas City. He led the Chiefs to an 11-5 season and their first division title in 22 years. He also earned his eighth selection to the Pro Bowl—his first as an AFC player.

most of them. Three times, he averaged at least 7 yards per carry in a season, and twice he averaged more than 20 yards per catch.

Explosive? Lenny Moore was a 191-pound stick of dynamite.

"I've never seen a ball carrier who could get in as much trouble as Lenny," said his teammate, Gary Kerkorian, "or one who could get out of it."

They called Moore the "Reading Rocket" when he arrived from Reading, Pennsylvania. By the time he caught pitchouts and passes from Johnny Unitas, they were calling him "Spats," a reference to the way he taped over his cleats. Moore was the NFL rookie of the year in 1956. He would go on to be a five-time all-pro, helping Baltimore to three Western Conference titles and two NFL championships.

If anything, success came too easily to Moore. "I still don't know why, but I was mainly a loafer," he once admitted.

Early on, he let his prodigious talents speak for his lack of work ethic. But that practice betrayed him when he suffered a broken kneecap in 1962 after being moved to halfback, and in 1963, when he had an appendectomy and suffered a severe head injury. Moore's production declined. Teammate Raymond Berry wrote him a letter saying he "should be ashamed for not doing more with his God-given talents."

After a stern conversation with coach Don Shula, Moore dedicated himself to a comeback. He finished the 1964 season with an NFL-best 20 touchdowns. When he retired three years later, Moore's well-rounded résumé included 5,174 rushing yards, 363 receptions, and 113 touchdowns (second in NFL history at the time).

LENNY MOORE

Flanker-Halfback
Baltimore (1956-1967)

Because the Colts of the late 1950s and early 1960s had such an abundance of offensive talent, Lenny Moore's opportunities for the spotlight were limited. But Moore made the

IN THE BEGINNING...
When Joe Montana was asked about the first magic moment in his remarkable NFL career, he pinpointed December 7, 1980. On that day, he rallied the 49ers from a 35-7 halftime deficit to a 38-35 overtime victory against the New Orleans Saints. "That was the beginning of things for us," said Montana, who would lead the 49ers to four Super Bowl titles.

MARION MOTLEY

Fullback
Cleveland (AAFC 1946-49)
Cleveland (NFL 1950-53)
Pittsburgh (1955)

Marion Motley's journey to the Pro Football Hall of Fame was one of the longest or shortest, depending on your interpretation. In a strictly physical sense, Motley came from right around the corner. He played football across the street from the present site of the football shrine, at Canton's McKinley High School.

In a more figurative sense, Motley's path was a lot longer. He didn't play pro football until he was 26, after a war-time stint in the Navy. And when he joined the Cleveland Browns of the All-America Football Conference in 1946, he became one of four African-Americans to break the sport's color barrier. That honor also earned him late hits and cheap shots from bigoted opponents.

But Motley would not be denied. A large, powerful running back who weighed 238 pounds, he also was a sure-handed receiver and a devastating pass blocker. His coach, Paul Brown, claimed Motley could have made the Pro Football Hall of Fame as a linebacker if he had concentrated solely on defense.

Motley was the AAFC's career rushing leader. And he lost no steam when the Browns joined the NFL in 1950, leading the senior league with 810 yards. "When he ran off tackle, players seemed to fly off him in all directions," Brown said. "And he could run away from linebackers and defensive backs, if he didn't trample them first."

ANTHONY MUÑOZ

Tackle
Cincinnati (1980-1992)

Many called it a gamble when the Bengals drafted Anthony Muñoz in the first round in 1980. Nobody denied that he was big (6-6, 278) and talented. But he had undergone three knee surgeries at USC. Was he durable enough for the NFL?

One-hundred-seventy-seven consecutive games and two Super Bowl appearances later, the answer no longer was in doubt. Muñoz missed one start during that stretch, but he entered that game on Cincinnati's second series.

Muñoz's career was about more than endurance. In every possible respect, he defined the position of offensive tackle. He was a freight train on running plays and a one-man force field on pass plays. Despite his size, he was incredibly agile. He was a reserve pitcher for USC's 1978 national-championship baseball team, and he caught 4 touchdown passes on tackle-eligible plays during his NFL career.

Muñoz earned 11 Pro Bowl bids, and the NFL Players Association named him offensive lineman of the year four times. In 1991, he won

perhaps his most cherished honor, the NFL Man of the Year award, for his off-field activities.

"Anthony is a better person than he was a player," said Sam Wyche, his former head coach. "And he was one of the greatest players of all time. This is what heroes are supposed to look and act like."

BRONKO NAGURSKI ▼

Fullback
Chicago Bears (1930-37, 1943)

After Bronko Nagurski became the first collegiate football player to be All-America at two positions (tackle and fullback), his coach, Minnesota's Doc Spears, told how he discovered the phenomenon. "I was driving by a farm," Spears said, "when I noticed this big farm boy plowing a field. I stopped for directions, and the boy picked up the plow and pointed with it."

It was difficult to separate fact from fiction in the life of Bronko Nagurski. One tale says he was forced out of bounds at full speed and flattened a policeman's horse. Another had him missing a tackle, careening into a Model T, and shearing off the fender.

At least one of the stories is documented: In 1943, the Bears signed Nagurski to fill a spot on their war-depleted roster—after he had been retired for five years. Nagurski returned, started mostly at tackle, and scored the go-ahead touchdown in the 1943 NFL title game.

The 225-pound Nagurski was a superb linebacker and an underrated passer, but it was his running style that proved hardest to forget.

"I had five stitches in my face," said Green Bay's Clarke Hinkle of the first time he tackled Nagurski. "My biggest thrill in football was the day he announced his retirement."

> " *My biggest thrill in football was the day [Nagurski] announced his retirement.* "
>
> *Clarke Hinkle*

JOE NAMATH
Quarterback
New York Jets (1965-1976)
Los Angeles (1977)

Because his career statistics are inconsistent at best—he completed barely 50 percent of his passes and threw 47 more interceptions than touchdowns—and his legend grand, there is a tendency to view Joe Namath as more flash than substance.

That would be a mistake. Behind the white shoes and the swinging bachelor lifestyle was a phenomenal passer.

Namath came to pro football with more than a little fanfare in 1965. His college coach, Alabama's Bear Bryant, called him "the greatest athlete I have ever coached." The New York Jets of the American Football League outbid the NFL's St. Louis Cardinals by agreeing to pay Namath the unheard-of sum of $427,000 over six years. The agreement marked the richest football contract ever consummated and a major salvo in the AFL-NFL war.

Broadway Joe did not disappoint his many admirers. He opened the 1965 season on the Jets' bench, but he ended it by playing in the AFL All-Star Game and collecting rookie-of-the-year honors. It only got better after that.

In 1967, Namath passed for 4,007 yards, a pro football record. The next season, he was named AFL player of the year after directing the Jets to an 11-3 record. He then passed for 3 touchdowns to propel the Jets to a 27-23 victory over the Raiders in the AFL Championship Game and set up a Super Bowl III showdown with the NFL-champion Baltimore Colts.

Super Bowl III is hailed as a turning point in pro football history, and Namath was at the eye of the storm. He made headline news by guaranteeing victory over heavily favored Baltimore. And he backed up his words with efficient passing and astute play-calling in a stunning 16-7 victory.

Unfortunately, the rest of Namath's body couldn't keep pace with his arm. He missed half of the Jets' games from 1970-73, and when he did play, his lack of mobility made him an easy target. His glory days were over by the time the leagues merged in 1970. But those who saw Namath in his prime remember a whip-like arm and a field leader who never quit.

ERNIE NEVERS

Fullback
Duluth (1926-27)
Chicago Cardinals (1929-1931)

When star halfback Red Grange signed with the New York Yankees of the upstart American Football League in 1926, the NFL rightfully worried about its future. Grange was a huge box-office draw. Could the older league hope to find an equally steady attraction?

The answer came in the form of Ernie Nevers, a ruggedly handsome fullback from Stanford. Nevers had outshone the famed Four Horsemen of Notre Dame in the 1925 Rose Bowl, though his team lost the game 27-10. After the next season, he signed with Ole Haugsrud, who had bought the Duluth (Minnesota) Eskimos for $1.

Haugsrud immediately dubbed his club "Ernie Nevers's Traveling Eskimos," and travel they did. Of the 29 games the Eskimos played in 1926, 28 were on the road. "The Iron Men of the North," as they were dubbed by Grantland Rice, traveled an estimated 17,000 miles in three months. And Nevers played 1,711 of a possible 1,740 minutes.

The man never slowed down. He ran track at Stanford, and he pitched for three years with the St. Louis Browns, giving up a home run to Babe Ruth and getting his first major-league hit against legendary Walter Johnson.

Nothing was beyond Nevers's abilities. He ran, passed, kicked, and tackled as well as anyone—even Jim Thorpe, who preceded him. "Nevers was better than Thorpe," said Pop Warner, who coached both in college. "He had more desire and determination, and he could do a lot of things that Thorpe couldn't do."

After sitting out the 1928 season with an injury, Nevers returned and had his greatest success with the Chicago Cardinals, including one season (1930) in which he served as player-coach. On Thanksgiving Day, 1929, he scored every point for the Cardinals in a 40-6 victory against the crosstown-rival Bears. That 40-point performance is the oldest surviving record in the *NFL Record & Fact Book.*

> *Nevers was better than Thorpe. He had more desire and determination and could do a lot of things that Thorpe couldn't do.*
>
> *Pop Warner*

EXTINCT FRANCHISE
The Duluth Eskimos (formerly Kelleys), whose uniform Ernie Nevers wore in 1926-27, suspended operation prior to the 1928 season, after only four seasons.

CLASSIC LINEBACKER
No player ever looked better cast as a middle linebacker than Ray Nitschke. But that isn't where he started out. He was a quarterback in high school and a running back at the University of Illinois.

> **"**
>
> *It's not so much his speed or even his quickness. It's a desire to make the play...to get to the right spot ahead of everybody else.*
>
> **"**
>
> *Les Richter*

RAY NITSCHKE
Linebacker
Green Bay (1958-1972)

Ray Nitschke was born to play football. He even looked the part: balding head, lantern jaw, eyes glaring, teeth on a shelf in his locker.

Most of all, he had a football temperament: a recklessness and an intensity that frightened teammates nearly as much as opponents. Yes, Ray Nitschke had just about everything a coach could want in a middle linebacker. He inspired and coaxed the Packers' defense to five NFL titles and two Super Bowls in the 1960s, and no one ever worked harder at it.

"It's not so much his speed or even his quickness," said Les Richter, a linebacker with the Rams. "It's a desire to make the play, an ability to get to the right spot ahead of everybody else."

Nitschke never was very far from the football. He intercepted 25 passes in his career. He was named most valuable player of the 1962 NFL Championship Game after recovering 2 fumbles and deflecting a pass in a 16-7 victory over the Giants. The game was played in wind-chill conditions of minus-20 degrees. That was classic Nitschke weather.

Nitschke's father died when he was 5, his mother when he was 13. Ray was raised by his brother Bob, who became his legal guardian. He was a wild soul until coach Vince Lombardi

came along to tame him with a recipe of tough love and strict discipline. What most fans never came to realize was that the snarling, growling, forearm-throwing Nitschke was a bespectacled puppy dog whenever he was away from the game that consumed him.

"Off the field, you hardly would have identified Ray as being a middle linebacker," teammate Bart Starr said. "He was meek and mild and easygoing, very respectful of others. He was a classic example of Doctor Jekyll and Mister Hyde."

NFL quarterbacks of the sixties would have preferred to see a little more Jekyll and a little less Hyde.

MERLIN OLSEN

Defensive Tackle
Los Angeles (1962-1976)

"A good defensive lineman must be part charging buffalo and part ballet dancer," Merlin Olsen once said. "And he must know when to be which. It's more an emotional state and an ability to concentrate. If you don't have those, you can't generate the horsepower."

Olsen's engine revved higher and longer than just about anyone else who played the game of football.

After winning the Outland Trophy at Utah State in 1961, Olsen arrived in the NFL with a reputation—and he quickly lived up to it. He earned his first start in the third preseason game of his rookie season and held the Rams' left defensive tackle spot until he retired after the 1976 season. In between, he missed only two games and finished with a streak of 198 starts.

Moreover, he played at a high level throughout his 15-year career. Olsen was voted Los Angeles's outstanding defensive player or most valuable player for six consecutive seasons, and he earned a league-record 14 Pro Bowl selections.

A massive figure (6-5, 270 pounds), Olsen did his job with brawn, to be certain. But he used his brains just as effectively. Olsen was Phi Beta Kappa as an undergraduate, and he later returned for a master's degree in finance. "He knew what was going on at all times," former coach George Allen said, "and took advantage of every weakness the opposition had and every mistake that was made."

Olsen played the first half of his career as part of the Rams' fabled "Fearsome Foursome" defensive line, along with Deacon Jones, Rosey Grier (later replaced by Roger Brown), and Lamar Lundy. During this phase, Olsen was the controlled and steady counterweight to Jones's wild-eyed pass rush.

Later in his career, Olsen was allowed to free-lance more. Either way, he was among the best and most consistent players in the league.

After his retirement, a new generation came to know him as Jonathan Garvey in the television series *Little House on the Prairie* and later as the title character in *Father Murphy*.

to six AFL or AFC Championship Games. He did it despite a medical file that included 10 broken noses, several concussions, and numerous surgeries on both knees.

"Jim loved to win," said teammate George Blanda. "He led by example and he set the tempo. He gave the Raiders an image of hard discipline, hard work, and hard-nosed football."

▼ALAN PAGE
Defensive Tackle
Minnesota (1967-1978)
Chicago (1978-1981)

Alan Page was unlike other defensive tackles. He ran marathons and studied nutrition. He lost weight even as his coaches implored him to bulk up. And when he was inducted into Hall of Fame in 1988, he selected a prominent educator, not a former coach, to introduce him.

▲JIM OTTO
Center
Oakland (1960-1974)

Here is a list of every player who was voted All-AFL at the center position during the 10 years of that league's existence: Jim Otto.

That's it. For the lifetime of the American Football League, Otto was unchallenged at his position. "Every year he was there, and every year he was all-pro," said Tom Flores, his teammate and and later a Raiders' assistant coach. "The coaches used to say, 'Well, Jim's at center, now who else do we have to vote on?'"

Otto was an undersized 205-pound center and linebacker at the University of Miami. At least partly because of his modest size, no NFL team ever expressed an interest in him. So he wound up in the fledgling AFL, playing for the Oakland Raiders, and he eventually bulked up to 255 pounds.

He was there for the Raiders' first snap in 1960, and he stuck around for 15 seasons. By the time he retired, Otto started 210 consecutive regular-season games–plus another 98 in the postseason and preseason–and helped his team

Page could afford to follow a unique path. Unbelievably swift, he played an aggressive style that had him shooting into the gaps as a play unfolded.

Page won a starting position in the fourth game of his rookie season and never was out of the lineup again. When he retired after the 1981 season, he put to rest a streak of 237 starts, including 218 in the regular season. He recovered 23 fumbles and blocked 28 kicks. Quarterback sacks were not officially recorded until 1982, but unofficial records show him with a whopping 173 for his career.

Page was the heart of Minnesota's renowned "Purple People Eaters" defensive line. But coach Bud Grant, tired of pleading, waived him when his weight dropped to 225 pounds. The Bears picked him up immediately, and Page never missed a down.

Chicago made the playoffs in 1979, Page's first full season with the club, repeating a theme previously borne out at Notre Dame and Minnesota. "Page might have been a great player," Bears coach Neill Armstrong said. "But even more, he had that ability to make average teams great teams."

After his football playing days came to an end, Page became a justice on the Minnesota Supreme Court.

JIM PARKER ▶
Guard-Tackle
Baltimore (1957-1967)

During training camp one year, Baltimore's Jim Parker sat down and composed a list of 19 personal goals for the upcoming season. Number one was, "Be the best offensive lineman on the field."

It was a heady aspiration, but Parker was up to the task. During his 11 NFL seasons, few could challenge the Ohio State product. George Allen, when he coached the Rams, claimed he gave up even attempting to pressure Colts quarterback Johnny Unitas from Parker's side of the line. "So all by himself he took away half of your pass rush," Allen said.

Parker played left tackle for more than five seasons. Then, in the middle of his sixth year, Baltimore coach Weeb Ewbank abruptly switched him to left guard. Parker hit the ground running, and at the end of the year was named all-pro at that position. That was one of eight such consecutive selections. He later became the first pure offensive lineman to be selected for enshrinement into the Pro Football Hall of Fame.

"If you were going to build an offensive lineman from scratch, Parker could be used as your model," said teammate Bob Vogel. "He embodied all the characteristics. He was big [6-3, 273], and he had exceptional strength and very good quickness."

JOB DESCRIPTION
Jim Parker didn't take long to learn his main task with the Colts. "Just keep everybody away from John [Unitas]," Parker said. "I remember coach Weeb Ewbank telling me, 'You will be the most unpopular man on the team if the quarterback is hurt.'"

WALTER PAYTON

Running Back
Chicago (1975-1987)

M ost football fans remember the yardage Walter Payton gained on the ground—an NFL-record 16,726—many of them coming in spectacular, airborne fashion. It's easy to forget that he also caught 492 passes, the standard for running backs when he retired. He also was a wicked blocker, and he threw 8 touchdown passes on halfback options.

Payton broke records in college, but because he did it for Jackson State, a small Division II school, he wasn't a household name when the Bears drafted him in the first round in 1975. But he was well-known by November 20, 1977, when he ran through the stunned Vikings for 275 yards on 40 carries. It stands as the greatest rushing performance in NFL history.

Payton stood only 5 feet 10 inches and weighed 202 pounds, but he was a workhorse back. He led the league in rushing attempts four consecutive years (1976-79), and his career total of 3,838 attempts is nearly 600 more than Emmitt Smith's second-place figure. Payton did the bulk of his running between the tackles, too. Yet in 13 seasons he missed only one game as a result of injury, and he swore it was only a coach's grudge that kept him out of that one.

Payton labored most of his career for mediocre teams. In 1985, the rest of the Bears finally caught up to him, helping him earn a victory ring in Super Bowl XX.

JERRY RICE
Wide Receiver
San Francisco (1985-present)

Joe Montana and Steve Young both set records and won titles while playing quarterback for the 49ers. Physically and stylistically, they were polar opposites. The right-handed Montana and the left-handed Young did have one thing in common: Jerry Rice, the most prolific receiver in NFL history.

Rice set 18 NCAA Division I-AA records at Mississippi Valley State. San Francisco coach Bill Walsh traded up to get him in the first round of the 1985 draft, and Rice ascended like a rocket.

In his third year, he set an NFL record with 22 touchdown receptions–in a season shortened by a players' strike. The next year, he was the MVP of Super Bowl XXIII, with 11 catches for 215 yards against the Bengals. In 1990, he had the first of his four 100-catch seasons.

Even beaten defenders have marveled at the production Rice has generated from subtle assets. He is big (6-2, 200), but not physically overpowering. He is fast, but many receivers are speedier. What sets him apart is his flawless route running.

"Most wide receivers, when they break in or out, they'll drop their shoulders or bend at the waist or bend at the knees," said cornerback Eric Davis, who has been both teammate and foe to Rice. "With Jerry, you couldn't tell whether he was going to run fifty yards, or five yards and stop."

Those mechanics have allowed Rice to rewrite the NFL records books. Entering the 2000 season, his career regular-season totals stood at 1,206 receptions for 18,442 yards and 169 touchdowns. His 124 postseason catches also were a record. He was miles ahead of the competition, and it was no accident.

"I think it would blow people away to know how hard Jerry works during the week," teammate Brent Jones said. "And I'm talking about people on other teams, not the fans."

> **"**
> *I think [Rice] believes that if they covered him with eleven guys, he should still be open and win the game.*
> **"**
>
> *Steve Young*

BARRY SANDERS

Running Back
Detroit (1989-1998)

When Barry Sanders suddenly announced his retirement prior to the 1999 NFL season, both fans and players were stunned beyond belief. Nobody wanted to believe they might have seen the last of the incomparable running back.

Some football players win respect from their peers. Sanders drew something closer to awe. "All you have to do is watch Barry run the ball once," running back Thurman Thomas said. "That's all. Just see him carry the ball one time, and you'll understand that the man does things with that football that I don't think anyone else can do."

Sanders was almost miniscule (5-8, 203) by NFL standards. But long-time defensive coach Floyd Peters swears Sanders was "a 280-pound man who was cut off at the knees and put his shoes back on."

Sanders's massive leg muscles gave him incredible balance and allowed him to change direction in a flash, while larger tacklers flowed by like a landslide. His carries from scrimmage had a tendency to look like cartoons. Once, against Buffalo, he spun on his hands and helmet, popped back onto his feet, and then continued downfield.

Sanders's decade with the Detroit Lions featured a string of successes. He rushed for more than 1,000 yards and was selected to the Pro Bowl in all 10 seasons. Four times, he led the NFL in rushing, including 1997, when he motored for 2,053—the second-best one-season total in the history of the league. He compiled those remarkable statistics, for the most part, while playing for average teams.

When Sanders walked away from football, he was on the doorstep of Walter Payton's all-time NFL rushing record. There was little doubt that he could surpass Payton's mark. But if there is one thing defenders learned about Sanders, it was not to try to guess where he was headed next.

As Detroit defensive tackle Jerry Ball said, "By the time you get to where Barry is, he's not there anymore."

DEION SANDERS

Cornerback-Kick Returner
Atlanta (1989-1993)
San Francisco (1994)
Dallas (1995-present)

Even those who disdain his showboat style find it hard to take their eyes off Deion Sanders, whether he is on the football field or the baseball diamond.

The man who called himself "Prime Time" qualifies as a ground-breaking athlete. He is the only man to play in both the World Series and the Super Bowl, and the only one to score an NFL touchdown and hit a major-league home run in the same week. Sanders once ran a leg of the 4x100-meter relay at Florida State, then jogged over to the baseball diamond in time to rap a game-winning hit.

More than anything, though, Sanders was meant to play pass defense. When the all-pro cornerback was performing at his peak, the Cowboys usually put him man-for-man on the opponent's best receiver, cheated their free safety to the opposite side of the field, and put their other defensive backs in zone coverage.

In effect, TV commentator John Madden said, "Deion is the first NFL player to be able to dominate and dictate a game from the defensive back position."

Quarterbacks rarely dared to challenge Sanders. He combined world-class speed and superior pass-catching skills (he even started at wide receiver in 1996). From any place on the field, he was a touchdown waiting to happen. Sanders finished the 1999 season with 18 career touchdowns on returns (the most ever), including 8 on interception returns, 6 on punt returns, 3 on kickoff returns, and 1 on a fumble recovery return.

Never lacking for self-confidence, Sanders has been chastised as a prima donna. But his teammates will tell you his image doesn't always jibe with the real person.

"There are things ya'll don't know about Deion because it doesn't get publicized," former teammate Nate Newton said. "He doesn't drink. He doesn't do drugs. He doesn't cuss. He's only flashy when he's out in the public entertaining."

"Yeah, the mud affected the kid," Chicago tight end Mike Ditka said. "If it had been dry out there, he would've scored ten touchdowns."

Sayers twice led the NFL in rushing (1966 and 1969), and he is the league's all-time leading kickoff returner (a 30.6-yard average). More than statistics, style separated Sayers from his peers. He brought bobbing, weaving excitement to his open-field scampers.

"Trying to bring Sayers down," said Lions defensive tackle Roger Brown, "is like going rabbit-hunting without a gun."

It wasn't long before Sayers's battered knees gave out. He underwent four surgeries and left the game after only 4½ healthy seasons. Pro Football Hall of Fame voters weren't dissuaded by his abbreviated career numbers, though. In 1977, they made Sayers, then 34, the youngest man ever enshrined.

JOE SCHMIDT ▶
Linebacker
Detroit (1953-1965)

In the summer of 1953, Gene Gedman and another Lions rookie walked into the office of Nick Kerbawy, the club's general manager. "Hello, Gene, how are you?" Kerbawy inquired. "Did you bring one of your fraternity brothers with you?"

"This is Joe Schmidt," Gedman said. "He was your seventh-round draft choice."

Though he played linebacker for three years at the University of Pittsburgh, Schmidt simply . did not look the part. He also had endured numerous injuries, which is why he lasted until the seventh round.

The Lions and the rest of the NFL would soon learn all about Schmidt, who became one of most respected players of his generation. In an era of great middle linebackers—including Ray Nitschke, Sam Huff, and Bill George—none surpassed Schmidt. He earned nine consecutive Pro Bowl selections (1954-1962 seasons), and was named the Lions' most valuable player four times.

Schmidt had a knack for reading plays before the snap, and was just as adept at getting to the point of attack. Once he arrived, he rarely missed a tackle. Relatively small (6-1, 222), he distinguished himself through tireless effort.

Trying to bring Sayers down is like going rabbit-hunting without a gun.

Roger Brown

▲ GALE SAYERS
Running Back
Chicago (1965-1971)

There was only one real problem with Gale Sayers's NFL career: It didn't last nearly long enough.

From the moment he stepped off the University of Kansas campus to play in the NFL in 1965, the "Kansas Comet" was something special. Hardened veterans could only shake their heads as the Bears' rookie led the league with 2,272 all-purpose yards and an NFL-record 22 touchdowns.

Included in that assault were a record-tying 6 touchdowns in a game against San Francisco at muddy Wrigley Field. Sayers's command performance featured an 80-yard reception, a 50-yard run, and an 85-yard punt return.

left tackle. Running primarily to their left, the Raiders rushed for a Super Bowl-record 266 yards. Marshall did not have a tackle.

"That was probably about as perfect a game as I've ever seen an offensive lineman play," said Tom Flores, then a Raiders' assistant.

And yet, it was not exactly a shocking development. From 1970, when he worked his way into Oakland's lineup, until 1982, Shell was the immovable object in silver and black. He played in eight Pro Bowls and helped his team to nine AFL or AFC championship games and two Super Bowl victories.

The Raiders noticed Shell at Maryland State-Eastern Shore because of his bulk (6-5, 285). But they also liked the fact that Shell played college basketball. He was exceptionally agile for his size.

He also was a quietly effective leader. "Whether you were his teammate or an opponent," said John Madden, Shell's head coach for 10 seasons, "you knew this was a man who deserved your deepest respect.

The Raiders respected Shell enough to make him the NFL's first modern-day African-American head coach, in 1989. And in 1990, he directed the Raiders to a division title.

"He always worked harder than anyone else," said teammate Wayne Walker. "After practice he would stay out on the field and run. And when I would walk by his room in training camp, he would always have his playbook out."

ART SHELL ▶

Tackle
Oakland-Los Angeles Raiders
(1968-1982)

Defensive end Jim Marshall was a two-time Pro Bowl selection and a key member of the Vikings' "Purple People Eaters" defense. In Super Bowl XI, he became the invisible man.

The man playing across the line from Marshall in that game was Art Shell, Oakland's

But playing for a bad team and two coaches who refused to build their offense around one player, Simpson never exceeded 800 rushing yards in his first three seasons. Lou Saban became Buffalo's head coach in 1972, and he quickly turned on "The Juice."

Simpson was the NFL's leading rusher four times in the next five years. Many believe his finest season was 1975, when he ran for 1,817 yards, gained another 426 on receptions, and scored a then-record 23 touchdowns.

Individual accomplishments came easy for Simpson, but his teams' cumulative record over 11 NFL seasons was a dismal 47-109-2. In 1976, he set a league mark with a 273-yard game against Detroit. Typically, the Bills lost 27-14.

MIKE ▶ SINGLETARY
Linebacker
Chicago (1981-1992)

Despite setting records for tackles at Baylor, Mike Singletary repeatedly heard that he was too small to play middle linebacker in the NFL because he stood barely 6 feet tall. He would never be able to see into the backfield, some scouts said.

Singletary was the youngest of 10 children in a preacher's home. He knew what it took to earn respect. Quiet and mannered off the field, he soaked up game plans like a sponge, and he chased down ball carriers without relent, his hawk-like eyes bulging. By the time he retired, Singletary had averaged more than 8 tackles a game, played in 10 Pro Bowls, and earned two NFL defensive player of the year awards (1985 and 1988). He missed only two games in 12 seasons with the Bears.

The Bears' defense in 1985 might have been the greatest ever. Pass rushers such as Richard Dent and Otis Wilson got most of the fans' attention, but it was the steady Singletary who powered the operation. He got his reward in Super Bowl XX, recovering 2 fumbles in a 46-10 rout of New England.

"Mike Singletary could kind of float along the line of scrimmage," said former quarterback Boomer Esiason. "You couldn't find him, and then all of a sudden—bam!—there he was in the chest of the ball carrier."

▲O.J. SIMPSON
Running Back
Buffalo (1969-1977)
San Francisco (1978-1979)

Orenthal James Simpson entered the final game of the 1973 season needing just 61 rushing yards to break Jim Brown's NFL single-season record of 1,863. The Bills were open about their game plan: Get Simpson his record.

He gained 57 yards before the Jets touched the ball. By the end of the snowy afternoon, he not only had eclipsed Brown's mark, he had become the first running back to break the 2,000-yard barrier.

Simpson was big (6-1, 212), shifty in the open field, and gifted with enough speed to have been a member of USC's world-record 440-yard relay team in college. He won the Heisman Trophy as a senior.

KICK RETURNER, TOO
Few fans remember that one of O.J. Simpson's primary duties in his first year was to return kicks for the Buffalo Bills. In 1969, he returned 21 kicks for an average of 25.2 yards per return. He added only 12 more returns for 461 yards in succeeding years, but his 30-yard career average remains the best in Bills history.

Smith was in the middle of a 19-sack season that helped the Bills to Super Bowl XXV, where he continued to shine, sacking Giants quarterback Jeff Hostetler for a safety.

Nimble and lean (6-4, 273), Smith earned recognition as of the quickest pass rushers in history. "He has an unbelievably explosive first step," said tackle Bruce Armstrong, a long-time opponent. "He's relentless, and once you get into him you must stay on him, because he has such great closing speed."

Smith, the first overall pick in the 1985 draft, was a Pro Bowl selection in 11 of his first 15 seasons. He entered the 2000 season with 171 career sacks—21½ behind NFL record holder Reggie White.

> " [Smith] has an unbelievably explosive first step. "
>
> *Bruce Armstrong*

BRUCE SMITH ▶

Defensive End
Buffalo (1985-1999)
Washington (present)

In 1990, Buffalo's Bruce Smith declared that he was the NFL's best defensive player. Some fans reacted negatively to the boast, but the defensive end was simply drawing attention to the double- and triple-team blocks that he seemed always to be confronting.

"I consider it an insult if it doesn't happen," he said. "I feel that the only way I'll get better is if I have at least two people on me."

It was difficult to argue with the big man.

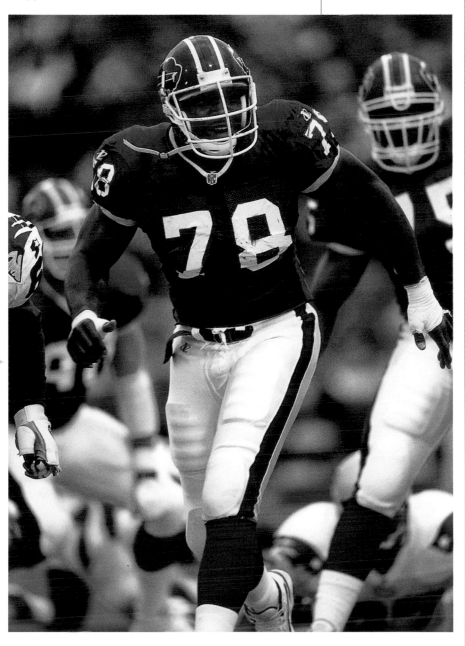

EMMITT SMITH

Running Back
Dallas (1990–present)

The knock against Emmitt Smith was that he lacked "breakaway speed." Did it really matter? As Whitey Jordan, his offensive coordinator at the University of Florida, said, "He may not go eighty yards on one play, but he can go forty yards twice."

After joining the Cowboys in 1990, Smith began posting gains of all different lengths. Mainly, though, the nifty running back became a pillar of consistency. He gained 937 yards as a rookie, and surpassed 1,000 in each of the next nine seasons.

How valuable was Smith to the best team of the 1990s? When he sat out the first two games in 1993, Dallas fell to 0-2. When he returned to the lineup, the Cowboys quickly rebounded to finish 12-4, then overpowered opponents in the postseason. At halftime of Super Bowl XXVIII, they trailed Buffalo 13-6. In the second half, they put the ball in Emmitt's hands, and he ran for 91 yards, finished with 132, and earned game MVP honors.

Smith always played considerably bigger than his size (5-9, 207). He rushed for an astronomical 8,804 yards at Escambia High School in Pensacola, Florida, then set 58 records in three years at Florida, where he gained 3,928 yards in three seasons.

He led the NFL in rushing four times between 1991 and 1995, including a personal-best 1,773 yards in 1995. He also scored a league-record 25 times that year, helping him attain the NFL's all-time career record for rushing touchdowns (136 through 1999).

The Cowboys' star running back never was better than in the final game of the 1993 season, when he rushed for 168 yards, caught passes for 61, and refused to leave the game even after suffering a separated shoulder.

"What separates him from other backs is explosiveness," Cowboys quarterback Troy Aikman explained. "Once he gets the ball, he has tremendous vision. He's hard to bring down because he's so strong in his hips and his legs."

The only place Smith is even stronger is in his heart.

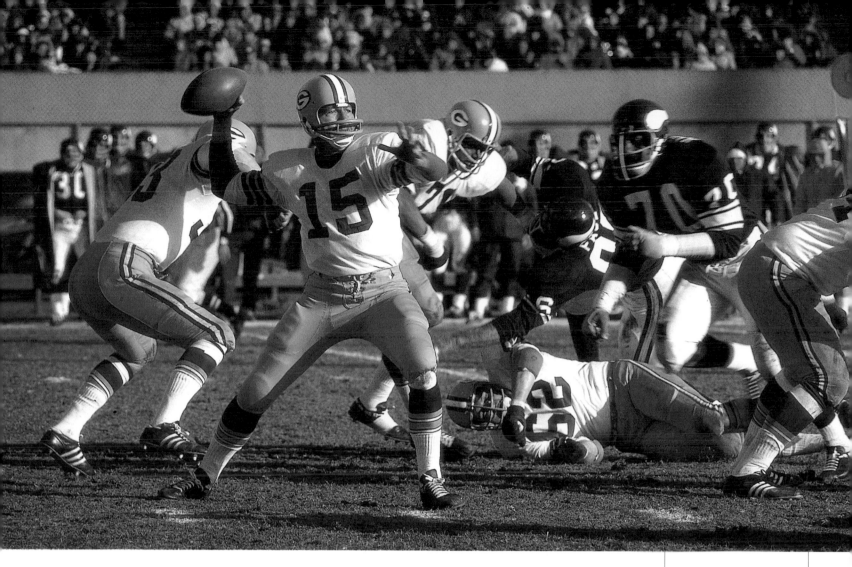

BART STARR

Quarterback
Green Bay (1956-1971)

Packers guard Jerry Kramer once was asked if he could think of anybody, in or out of football, who didn't like quarterback Bart Starr. "Nobody," Kramer replied, "except maybe me. Sometimes he irritates me."

"Why?" the reporter wondered.

"Because he's too perfect," Kramer said.

Whether he was passing downfield or attending a board meeting, Starr didn't make many mistakes. It may have hurt his reputation as a quarterback. He wasn't dashing. He rarely led last-second comebacks because he usually had Green Bay comfortably ahead. All he did was win. He took the Packers to an 82-24-4 record from 1960-67, during which time they won five NFL titles and two Super Bowls.

Against the Chiefs in Super Bowl I, a game that buzzed with rivalry and pressure, the Packers converted 11 of 14 third-down plays

with Starr at the controls. He attempted 7 third-down passes and completed 6. He finished the game with 16 completions in 23 attempts for 250 yards, earning the first of two consecutive MVP awards.

That was par for the course for Starr in the postseason. His regular-season statistics have been eclipsed by modern quarterbacks, but nobody can touch his postseason passer rating of 104.8. Joe Montana is in second place, nearly 10 points behind.

Starr was a long shot from the beginning. He came to Green Bay as a seventeenth-round draft pick from Alabama, then made the team by out-studying his competitors at quarterback. Vince Lombardi made him the starter when he arrived in 1959, and Starr eventually ran the offense so flawlessly that he once attempted a record 294 passes without an interception. He led the NFL in passing three times.

After Lombardi's Packers won their first title in 1961, receiver Gary Knafelc examined the ring commemorating the accomplishment. "On this championship ring it says, 'Dedication and Character,'" he noted. "This ring could have been designed for Bart Starr."

> " On this championship ring it says, 'Dedication and Character.' This ring could have been designed for Bart Starr. "
>
> *Gary Knafelc*

bench to lead Dallas to 17 fourth-quarter points and a 30-28 playoff victory over San Francisco. In the 1975 postseason, he beat Minnesota with the famed "Hail Mary" pass to Drew Pearson. Appropriately, he resurrected the Cowboys from a 13-point deficit to beat the arch-rival Redskins in his final regular-season game.

Staubach won the Heisman Trophy at Navy, but the Cowboys had to wait four years while he completed his tour of duty. He joined the team as a 27-year-old rookie, and he didn't start full time until his third season. When he finally assumed control of the offense in 1971, Staubach led the NFL in passing (the first of four titles) and finished the season as the most valuable player of Super Bowl VI.

▼ERNIE STAUTNER

Defensive Tackle
Pittsburgh (1950-1963)

Ernie Stautner, a Bavarian immigrant, injured his ankles so badly playing football in grade school that he had to see a doctor. This was bad news for a family barely able to pay its bills.

FAVORITE TARGET
No one was on the receiving end of more of Roger Staubach's passes than Drew Pearson (above), who led the Cowboys in receptions from 1974-77.

▲ROGER STAUBACH

Quarterback
Dallas (1969-1979)

Quarterback Roger Staubach was a walking contradiction—a button-down Naval officer who played football with abandon.

"Roger never knew when the game was over," tight end Billy Joe DuPree said. "At the end of the game, even if we were down by twenty points, he'd be standing there by himself trying to figure out a way we could win it."

He often found a way. On 23 occasions, Staubach led the Cowboys to a fourth-quarter comeback, 14 times in the final two minutes. Some of the rallies were epic.

In 1972, after missing much of the season with a separated shoulder, he came off the

Stautner's father sternly told his son, *"Keine mehr Fussbal. Keine mer yamerung."* Translation: *No more football. No more complaining.*

Ernie only adhered to the second command, playing secretly for years while keeping his injuries hidden. Local newspapers began to recount his exploits, but Ernie's parents could not read English. The deception finally ended when Stautner made the all-Albany (New York) team as a senior in high school and his picture appeared in the newspaper. "What could he do then but be proud?" the younger Stautner said.

Stautner starred at Boston College as a 235-pound defensive tackle. The Giants told him he was too small, so he signed with Pittsburgh. During the next 14 years he became the most respected player on a tough, but unsuccessful, team. He was a battler who made nine Pro Bowls and played through a litany of injuries.

"The man ain't human," Colts tackle Jim Parker said. "He's too strong to be human."

Stautner had forearms like pile drivers. They were the result, he said, of chopping tons of hay with an old scythe. "People are always saying they love the smell of new-mown hay," he confided. "Not me. I hate it."

But he loved football, and Steelers fans loved Stautner.

DWIGHT ▶ STEPHENSON

Center
Miami (1980-87)

Invariably, reporters would converge around Dwight Stephenson's locker after a victory, hoping to learn how the center had handled that day's ornery defensive tackles. Stephenson would politely give them clichés and one-word answers until Roy Foster, the guard who played (and dressed) next to him, would demand, "Come on, Dwight! Tell the folks something!"

It just wasn't in Stephenson's nature. He preferred to let his work do his talking, and it said volumes. He started for the Dolphins as a rookie and earned five consecutive Pro Bowl selections, beginning with the 1983 season.

"Make one mistake," the Jets' Joe Klecko said, "and Dwight would make a complete fool out of you."

Stephenson was so timid as a child that "even the girls would push me around." He built himself up with supermarket work and basketball, and developed his football skills to the point that he earned a scholarship to Alabama. It was legendary coach Paul (Bear) Bryant who moved him to center. Stephenson helped lead the Crimson Tide to consecutive national titles.

His teams kept winning in the NFL. The Dolphins made it to two Super Bowls in three years in the early 1980s. Each time they did it with a young quarterback (first David Woodley, then Dan Marino), both of whom benefited from great pass protection. That protection started with Dwight Stephenson.

FRONT AND CENTER
The Miami Dolphins can trace their history only to 1966, when they came to life as an AFL expansion team. But they already have produced two Hall of Fame centers—Jim Langer, who played from 1970-79, and Dwight Stephenson. Langer was inducted in 1987, Stephenson in 1998.

FRAN TARKENTON

Quarterback
Minnesota (1961-66, 1972-78)
New York Giants (1967-1971)

When football fans close their eyes and think of Fran Tarkenton, they still can see him running in crazy arcs and loops behind the line of scrimmage, a gang of angry pass rushers in pursuit, then heaving a pass downfield to a suddenly open receiver.

His Chaplinesque scrambles enthralled fans, exhausted overweight linemen, and exasperated his first coach, Norm Van Brocklin. They also helped win a lot of football games.

Tarkenton's first victory was one of his greatest. Leading the expansion Vikings in their first game in 1961, he lit up the scoreboard with 4 touchdown passes and ran for another score to stun the Chicago Bears 37-13. Suddenly, a nation of NFL fans knew about the dynamic quarterback from Georgia.

Unfortunately, Tarkenton was surrounded by little talent in his early years in Minnesota, or in New York, where he went when the Giants traded two first-round and two second-round draft choices for his services in 1967. During his first 11 seasons, his teams had a winning record only twice.

Tarkenton returned to the Vikings in 1972 and found a strikingly different situation. Now surrounded with a full complement of offensive and defensive talent, he guided Minnesota to six division titles and three Super Bowls in seven seasons. He ran to keep opponents off balance, not to preserve his health.

Tarkenton, who never hesitated to throw deep, wound up with some remarkable passing numbers. When he retired after the 1978 season, he owned NFL career records for attempts (6,467), completions (3,686), yards (47,003), and touchdown passes (342). Dan Marino later surpassed those marks. But Marino made his place in history solely with his arm. Tarkenton added 3,674 rushing yards and 32 rushing touchdowns to his résumé.

Tarkenton was selected to nine Pro Bowls in his 18-year career. After leading the NFC in passing in 1975, he was named NFL player of the year.

CHARLEY TAYLOR

Wide Receiver-Running Back
Washington (1964-1975, 1977)

When Charley Taylor came out of Arizona State, the question was not *if* he could play in the pros, but *where* he would play.

"I cannot remember anyone coming out of college who had all the credentials and ability that Charley Taylor had," said Don Klosterman, who was general manager of the AFL's Chiefs in 1964. "My first evaluation was that he would be an all-pro defensive corner, that he'd be a great running back, and an exceptional flanker and kick runner. And maybe also coach a little."

Washington drafted Taylor and lined him up at halfback, but he was hard to pigeonhole. He rushed for 755 yards, gained 814 on receptions, and was named NFL rookie of the year. But in the seventh game of 1966, the Redskins permanently switched Taylor from running back to wide receiver.

"I wasn't totally for the move at first," he said, "but I grew to love it."

Defensive backs despised it. Capitalizing on his superior all-around athletic skills and some tricks he had learned in the backfield, Taylor became one of the NFL's premier wide receivers. He led the league in receptions in each of his first two seasons at the new position. He caught 50 or more passes seven times and was selected to eight Pro Bowls, retiring with an NFL-record 649 receptions for 9,110 yards and 90 total touchdowns.

Ermal Allen, the Cowboys' long-time assistant coach, once called Taylor "the best blocking wide receiver I've seen since I've been in professional football."

That was part of his aggressive approach. "He was physical, an intimidator," former Dallas safety Cliff Harris said. "Most receivers aren't like that. They're passive and try to stay on the good side of defensive backs. But Taylor would try to intimidate you physically and mentally. He'd try to hurt you."

> **"**
> *[Taylor] was physical, an intimidator. Most receivers aren't like that.*
> **"**
>
> *Cliff Harris*

JIM TAYLOR
Fullback
Green Bay (1958-1966)
New Orleans (1967)

The Lombardi-era Packers won their second consecutive title on a frozen field in New York, where they outlasted the Giants 16-7 in the 1962 NFL Championship Game. On a day when the wind-chill factor crept below zero, Green Bay's Jim Taylor carried 31 times and pounded out 85 yards. After the game, Giants linebacker Sam Huff still could not believe it.

"No human being could have stood the punishment he got today," Huff said of Taylor. "Every time he was tackled it was like crashing him down on a sidewalk. But he kept bouncing up and snarling at us and asking for more."

For a decade, Taylor was football's ultimate fullback. He was only average size (6-0, 216), but he was strong, tough, and determined. He dished out as many blows as he received.

Taylor played in the shadow of Cleveland's Jim Brown, who clearly had the upper hand as an all-around runner. But Taylor was better as a blocker and on short-yardage plays. Taylor also notched one running feat that neither Brown nor any other runner had accomplished to that point, gaining 1,000 yards in five consecutive seasons (1960-64). In 1962, Taylor scored an NFL-record 19 touchdowns.

It was a surprising success story for a poor kid from Baton Rouge, Louisiana. Taylor's father died when he was in grammar school. The youngster went to work for an oil pipe company in high school, swinging a heavy hammer and handling massive pipes atop an oil rig. Compared to that, battling Sam Huff and Joe Schmidt was easy work.

"Football is really a matter of inches," Taylor said. "When it comes to getting those inches, it's between me and the defense. And no one is going to hit me harder than I hit them."

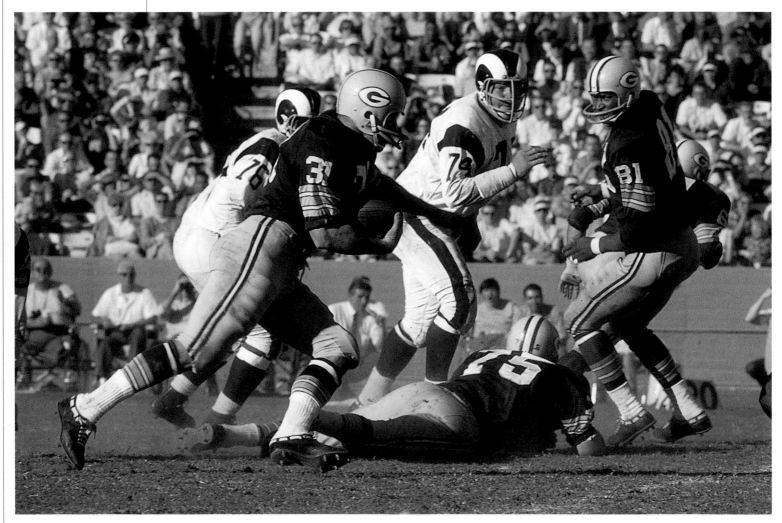

LAWRENCE TAYLOR

Linebacker
New York Giants (1981-1993)

Just about every year some hotshot collegiate defensive prospect is referred to as "the next Lawrence Taylor." No one has scaled those heights yet.

"When God was creating pass-rushing linebackers," former Giants coach Bill Parcells said, "he had Lawrence Taylor in mind."

Taylor revolutionized his position. Other linebackers had proved themselves adept as pass rushers, but they did so with occasional blitzes, and most of them could be blocked by a willing fullback. The idea of negating Taylor with a back was ludicrous. He demanded the attention of an opponent's best tackle, and usually an extra blocker. Offensive game plans were designed solely with Taylor in mind.

"He had a relentlessness that was unmatched," said quarterback Joe Theismann. "He was the only defensive player I can remember who we had to design our game plan around. The first question at our meeting was, 'How are we going to handle Lawrence?'"

No one ever found an adequate answer.

Taylor was a sack machine. In 1986, he recorded 20½ sacks en route to becoming the first linebacker named NFL MVP by the *Associated Press*. He played in 10 Pro Bowls and retired second on the all-time list with 132½ sacks (which didn't include his 9½ as a rookie, the year before sacks became an official statistic).

Taylor's value went far beyond statistics, though. His unflagging energy helped propel the Giants to seven playoff appearances and victories in Super Bowls XXI and XXV. He opened the door to that second title when he recovered a 49ers' fumble to set up Matt Bahr's winning field goal in the waning moments of the 1990 NFC Championship Game.

"He was the catalyst," Parcells said. "He inspired the other players, he inspired the other coaches, he inspired me."

GUESS WHO?
Few quarterbacks who played in the 1980s were unfamiliar with Lawrence Taylor (above), but he was especially recognizable to Randall Cunningham and Ron Jaworski of the Philadelphia Eagles. Before Taylor retired in 1993, he sacked each of them 12½ times.

▼ JIM THORPE

Back
Canton (1920, 1926)
Cleveland (1921)
Oorang (1922-23)
Rock Island (1924)
New York Giants (1925)
Chicago Cardinals (1928)

Jim Thorpe's Indian name was Wa-Tho-Huk. It means "Bright Path." On anyathletic field, Thorpe blazed a glorious trail.

A member of the Sac-and-Fox tribe, with some French and Irish blood, Thorpe was born in a one-room cabin in Prague, Oklahoma. From those humble roots he went on to win the pentathlon and the decathlon at the 1912 Olympic Games in Sweden. (The International Olympic Committee stripped him of his medals after learning he had been paid while playing semipro baseball, but restored them posthumously in 1982.) He also played major-league baseball, but many think of him first and foremost as a football player.

Thorpe was at his best playing for the Canton Bulldogs in the years before the NFL was formed. He did everything well— running, passing, kicking, catching, tackling—and upon his shoulders the Bulldogs won unofficial pro football titles in 1916, 1917, and 1919.

Renowned Notre Dame coach Knute Rockne, who played for Massillon, once found himself prone after trying to tackle Thorpe. "It was as if a locomotive had hit me," Rockne said, "and then been followed by a ten-ton truck rambling over the remains."

Thorpe was so popular that when the APFA (forerunner to the NFL) was formed in 1920, organizers made him the figurehead president. He remained a dependable gate attraction as an NFL player for eight seasons. Even past his prime, Wa-Tho-Huk was one of the league's most talented players.

▲ EMLEN TUNNELL

Safety
New York Giants (1948-1958)
Green Bay (1959-1961)

In 1967, Emlen Tunnell became the first African-American and first pure defensive player to enter the Hall of Fame, an amazing culmination to a once-moribund career.

Tunnell suffered a broken vertebra in his neck while practicing during his freshman year at Toledo. Doctors told him that he never would play football again. Tunnell served a three-year stint in the Coast Guard, then enrolled at the University of Iowa, where he won a starting job on defense.

That wasn't enough for Tunnell. He wanted to play offense, so he walked into the New York Giants' offices and walked out with a contract. The Giants made him a safety, though they referred to him as their "offense on defense."

"With Em on defense," Giants coach Steve Owen said, "we have the potential to get the ball on any play in the game."

Tunnell also was one of the league's best kick returners. In 1952, he returned 30 punts for 411 yards, 15 kickoffs for 364 yards, and 7 interceptions for 149 yards. He scored 10 touchdowns in his career, and he still ranks as the NFL's all-time leader in interception-return yardage (1,282) and ranks second in career interceptions (79).

When Vince Lombardi became the Packers' head coach in 1959, he obtained Tunnell in a trade. The savvy veteran helped Green Bay to the NFL title in 1961.

CLYDE ▶ (BULLDOG) TURNER

Center-Linebacker
Chicago Bears (1940-1952)

The Chicago Bears thought they were on to something when they found Clyde (Bulldog) Turner at tiny Hardin-Simmons College in Abilene, Texas. But when they sent the senior a questionnaire, he responded, "I do not want to play professional football."

Skeptical of those sentiments, Bears owner George Halas made Turner his first pick in the 1940 draft. It turned out that Detroit's owner had paid Turner $200 to "get his teeth fixed" and reject other teams' offers. But Detroit's coach had neglected to draft Turner. The owner fired the coach, who revealed the payoff. The Lions were fined $5,000 for tampering, and the Bears got a sensational center and linebacker.

Turner was big for his day (6-2, 235), and also was fast and smart. It is said he studied all 11 assignments for any given play. That work ethic came in handy during a game in 1944, when some teammates were ejected for fighting. Turner had to play halfback, and he carried the ball once—for a 48-yard touchdown.

A six-time all-pro, Turner broke Mel Hein's eight-year reign as the all-NFL center. On defense, Turner intercepted 4 passes in five NFL title games, returning 1 for 20 yards and a touchdown in the Bears' 73-0 victory over Washington in 1940. He led the league with 8 interceptions in 1942, and turned in what he described as his favorite play in 1947, when he intercepted a pass thrown by Sammy Baugh and returned it 96 yards for a touchdown.

As teammate George Musso, a fellow member of the Hall of Fame, said of Bulldog, "Who knows what kind of player he would have been if he ever got to rest during a game?"

> **"**
> *Who knows what kind of player he would have been if he ever got to rest during a game?*
> **"**
>
> *George Musso*

JOHNNY UNITAS

Quarterback
Baltimore (1956-1972)
San Diego (1973)

The story has entered the realm of lore, like Babe Ruth's called shot and Jack Dempsey's fights. The Baltimore Colts got Johnny Unitas, arguably the greatest quarterback in history, for the price of an 80-cent phone call.

A year earlier, Unitas had been cut by his hometown team, the Pittsburgh Steelers. He spent the 1955 fall season earning $6 a game for a semipro team called the Bloomfield Rams. Understandably, he jumped at the Colts' offer. He was starting by the fifth game of 1956, and he didn't give up the job until he was traded to the Chargers in 1973.

Stoop-shouldered and unathletic in appearance, Unitas didn't look formidable until he got a football in his hands. Then his talent was unmistakable.

"He can throw short, long, hard, soft, on either side of you to keep it away from a defensive back, and he can throw it away when he has to," said Raymond Berry, Unitas's favorite receiver.

But Johnny U.'s arm always was secondary to his unnerving toughness. No matter how bloodied or trampled he was, Unitas always got up.

Merlin Olsen, the long-time defensive tackle for the Rams, once described what it was like to pursue Unitas after the quarterback had been nailed a few times. "Out of the corner of his eye, he may see you coming again," Olsen said. "And I swear that when he does, he holds the ball a split-second longer than he really needs to—just to let you know he isn't afraid of any man. Then he throws it on the button."

Unitas retired with NFL records for passing yards (40,239) and touchdowns (290). He once passed for touchdowns in 47 consecutive games, a record that remains unchallenged.

Unitas took Baltimore to NFL titles in 1958, 1959, and 1970. The 1958 title game is regarded as a turning point for the league. And no image dominates like Unitas leading the Colts down the field, first to tie the game in regulation, then to win it in overtime.

GENE UPSHAW

Guard
Oakland (1967-1981)

During Super Bowl II, as Oakland battled Green Bay, Raiders rookie guard Gene Upshaw kept soliciting advice from his veteran opponent, the Packers' Henry Jordan. "That kid was in there asking me what he did wrong," Jordan said afterward, "and all he did was kick the hell out of me. I kept asking myself, 'What if he does something right?'"

Upshaw, a quick study, soon did just about everything right. He wound up playing in seven Pro Bowls or AFL All-Star Games.

Not coincidentally, the Raiders followed right along. During Upshaw's 15 years with the Raiders, they made the playoffs 11 times and won Super Bowls XI and XV. He is the only man to play in the Super Bowl in three decades (1960s, 1970s, and 1980s).

Upshaw was a relative greenhorn when Oakland drafted him. He played only one year in high school and faced lesser competition at Texas A&I. But Oakland needed a guard with the physical stature to handle Chiefs defensive tackle Buck Buchanan. Upshaw was that man.

He was larger (6-5, 255) than most men at his position but just as fast as the smaller guys. What set him apart, though, were his leadership skills. He was a team captain, whom Raiders owner Al Davis called "Gov," joking that Upshaw would be governor of California some day. In 2000, he was re-elected as executive director of the NFL Players Association.

Old-timers remember Upshaw's hulking figure leading the Raiders' sweeps around left end. "When [stadiums] went to artificial turf, which made him faster," said broadcaster Charlie Jones, "it should have been illegal for him to lead a sweep."

NUMBER ONE
Few players have known all-or-nothing pressure the way Gene Upshaw did. He played in three AFL and seven AFC Championship Games during his 15-year pro football career.

> *When [stadiums] went to artificial turf, which made him faster, it should have been illegal for him to lead a sweep.*
>
> Charlie Jones

NORM VAN BROCKLIN

Quarterback
Los Angeles (1949-1957)
Philadelphia (1958-1960)

The image of a pro football quarterback is the tall and stoic figure who bravely leads his team, but says little more than "…on three."

Norm Van Brocklin, the fiery Dutchman, was the antithesis.

"He'd spit in your eye, call you every name in the book, then run your butt off the field," said Sam Huff, a middle linebacker who had his share of run-ins with Van Brocklin. "We used to hit him some wicked shots, and he'd say, 'Is this as hard as you can hit, Sweetie?' I loved him."

Van Brocklin was a junior at Oregon when he wrote to the Rams, saying he was ready to graduate early if they wanted to draft him. They did, in the fourth round in 1949, and he was a steal.

Van Brocklin led the NFL in passing in 1950, 1952, and 1954. Playing against an overmatched New York Yanks team in 1951, he set an NFL record that still stands by passing for 554 yards.

He loved to throw deep and often. But Van Brocklin was much prouder of the fact that, in his 12-year NFL career, five of his teams finished in first place and only two had losing records. In the 1951 title game he hit Tom Fears with a 73-yard touchdown pass in the fourth quarter, delivering a 24-17 victory for the Rams, their only championship prior to winning Super Bowl XXXIV.

Weary of quarterback controversies—Los Angeles alternated him first with Bob Waterfield, then with Bill Wade—Van Brocklin announced his retirement in 1957. He changed his mind when the Rams traded him to the Eagles. The 1960 season wound up being his finest moment. He led Philadelphia to a 17-13 victory over Vince Lombardi's Packers in the NFL Championship Game, then passed for 3 touchdowns in the Pro Bowl.

Van Brocklin left as he had arrived—in grand style.

GO DEEP!
Few quarterbacks were fonder of the long pass than Norm Van Brocklin, as evidenced by three Rams records he still holds: yards gained per pass attempt for a game (15.4), season (10.14), and career (8.49).

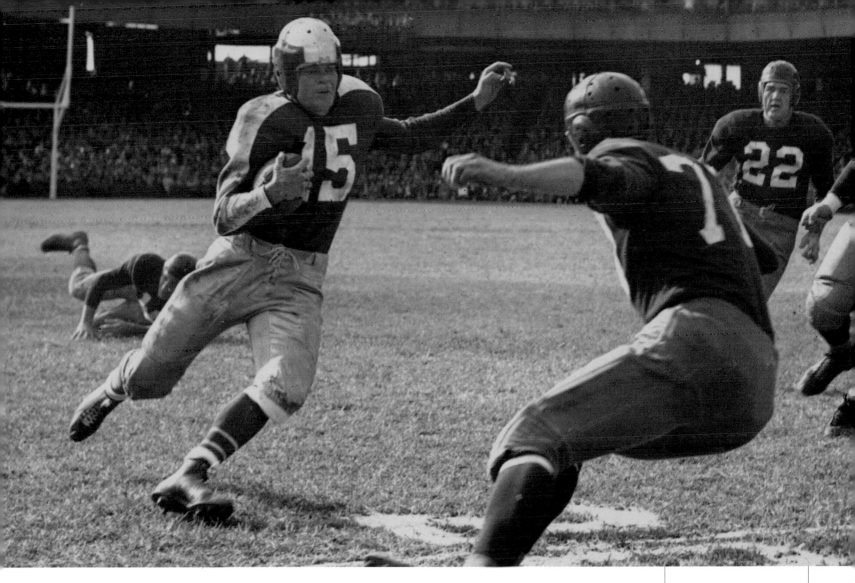

STEVE VAN BUREN

Halfback
Philadelphia (1944-1951)

Before Steve Van Buren arrived in 1944, the Eagles never finished higher than fourth place. With Van Buren, they became the most powerful football team of the late 1940s.

"He was our paycheck," said teammate Bucko Kilroy. "As he went, the Eagles went."

They usually went quite well. Philadelphia played in three consecutive NFL title games from 1947-49, winning the latter two. Each was testament to Van Buren's importance, and to his determination. In 1948, he outrushed the entire Chicago Cardinals team and scored the only touchdown on a snow-covered field for a 7-0 victory. In the 1949 title game, he ran for 196 yards on 31 carries to help beat the Rams 14-0 in ankle-deep mud at the Los Angeles Coliseum.

Van Buren was the first NFL back to lead the league in rushing three consecutive years, and the first to post two 1,000-yard seasons.

He was born in La Ceiba, Honduras, where his father was a fruit inspector. Orphaned at a young age, Van Buren lived in New Orleans with his grandparents. He was cut from his high school team as a 125-pound sophomore, but returned after two years of working in an iron foundry and won a scholarship to Louisiana State.

Van Buren was a physical marvel. In a 50-yard dash, teammates said, he could outrun teammate Clyde (Smackover) Scott, who was a silver-medal hurdler in the 1948 Olympics and was reputed to be the NFL's fastest player. But Van Buren also was a muscular 200-pounder who could knock linebackers flat.

He also was a good defensive back and an excellent kick returner. Van Buren could do anything, really, except pass. That wasn't part of what he considered a man's game.

"The fellow who threw the first pass," he said, "must have been someone too tired to run with the ball."

> **The fellow who threw the first pass must have been someone too tired to run with the ball.**
>
> *Steve Van Buren*

Warfield grew up dreaming of football in the steel-mill town of Warren, Ohio. Every summer, he drove to Hiram to watch the Browns at training camp. An All-America halfback at Ohio State, he was courted by both Cleveland and the AFL's Buffalo Bills. Buffalo offered more money, but Warfield signed with his favorite team.

After six seasons, the Browns traded him to the Dolphins for a first-round draft choice. Warfield's timing was perfect. He was in Miami for three consecutive Super Bowls, including victories in VII and VIII.

After one year with Memphis of the World Football League, Warfield returned to Cleveland. He didn't have to worry about acceptance. Three years earlier, wearing a Dolphins' uniform, he received a five-minute standing ovation by 80,000 fans in Cleveland Stadium.

MIKE ▶ WEBSTER

Center
Pittsburgh (1974-1988)
Kansas City (1989-1990)

Picture Mike Webster on a frigid day in Three Rivers Stadium, when sensible men are bundled head to toe. He was dressed in black short sleeves, biceps bulging.

"Webby was the first center to bring attention to the position," former linebacker Matt Millen said. "He was the first one with muscles. You noticed him because he was the first guy out of the huddle and he plopped over the ball with those big ol' arms."

Everyone figured Webster was the most powerful player in football. He made it official in 1980 when he won the "NFL's Strongest Man" competition.

But Webster did more than look the part. He played in nine Pro Bowls and helped the Steelers to four Super Bowl titles, starting the second two (XIII and XIV). The man from Tomahawk, Wisconsin, played 177 consecutive games until he suffered a dislocated elbow in 1986. He once handled every offensive snap for six consecutive seasons. He played more games (220) than anyone else in Steelers history, then went on to play 25 games for Kansas City.

▲ PAUL WARFIELD

Wide Receiver
Cleveland (1964-69, 1976-77)
Miami (1970-74)

Call it good fortune or misfortune, Paul Warfield was destined to play for teams that relied on great running backs. In Cleveland, he played with the immortal Jim Brown, then with Leroy Kelly. When he joined the Miami Dolphins, he was teammates with Larry Csonka and Eugene (Mercury) Morris.

As a result, Warfield's career total of 427 receptions is not eye-popping. But he made the most of them, averaging 20.1 yards per catch and scoring 85 touchdowns. Those who played with or against him know that he was a nearly perfect NFL receiver.

TOUCHDOWN MAKER
Paul Warfield had only one season in which he made more than 50 receptions, but he knew how to make the most of his catches. He led the league in touchdown receptions in both 1968 (12) and 1971 (11). And his career total of 85 touchdowns equates to an average of about 1 for every 5 receptions.

Far from being all brawn, Webster made the line calls for Pittsburgh's complex, trap-crazy running game. (Line calls are the linemen's blocking assignments, based on the defensive formation.) "He'd recognize a defense and turn around and suggest an audible," linemate Craig Wolfley said. "You don't see that very often."

White haunted quarterbacks throughout his career. He set records for career sacks (192½) and sacks in a Super Bowl (3 in game XXXI), and he fell 1 sack shy of the single-season mark when he tallied 21 in 1987, a strike-shortened season in which he played only 12 games.

"He's a guy you definitely want on your side rather than against you," said Packers quarterback Brett Favre.

Favre would know. A year before they became teammates, White slightly separated Favre's shoulder. The defender probably prayed for him that night. White, an ordained pastor, was hailed as the Minister of Defense. Always outspoken, often controversial, he was a man who lived his convictions.

"He is probably the most unselfish team player I've ever been around, and it rubs off," defensive coordinator Fritz Shurmur said. "If you were to look at one guy whose demeanor and whose mode of living is an example to all of us, it's Reggie White."

> **"**
> *[Reggie] is probably the most unselfish team player I've ever been around, and it rubs off.*
> **"**
>
> *Fritz Shurmur*

REGGIE ▶ WHITE

Defensive End
Philadelphia (1985-1992)
Green Bay (1993-98)

In 1992, Mike Holmgren's first season as head coach of the Packers, his defense ranked twenty-third in the league in yards allowed. The next season, Green Bay jumped to second.

"We went from twenty-three on defense to two," Holmgren said, "with no dramatic personnel changes, except for one man."

That man was Reggie White, probably the best all-around defensive end ever to wear an NFL uniform. Big (6-5, 291), strong, and agile,

LARRY WILSON

Safety
St. Louis (1960-1972)

Cardinals safety Larry Wilson once suffered a collapsed lung in a game, then came back to play two weeks later. No wonder quarterback Bobby Layne said, "Larry Wilson may have been the toughest guy, pound for pound, who ever played this game."

A seventh-round draft choice from Utah who never fully believed his job was safe—though he made the Pro Bowl eight times in 13 seasons—Wilson played through a variety of breaks, sprains, and migraines.

In 1965, he played with two broken hands, both of them bound in splints. Somehow, he intercepted a pass against Pittsburgh and returned it 34 yards for a touchdown while cradling the ball like a loaf of bread.

"With his hands like that, he couldn't wrap his arms around a ball carrier," said teammate Jerry Stovall. "So Larry tried to butt them down, like a goat. Finally he got sliced across the forehead. I looked at him, with two broken hands and blood running down his face. I said, 'Man, get out of here.'

"Larry said to me, 'Let's turn the ball over on the next play and I'll get off.'"

Wilson was of modest size (6-0, 190), but he took on blockers of any size on running plays. And he made an even greater impact against the pass. He led the NFL with 10 interceptions in 1966, and retired with a club-record 52.

Wilson was the first great practitioner of the safety blitz. St. Louis assistant coach Chuck Drulis designed the tactic, and Wilson perfected it, forcing opponents to keep a back in to block. He absorbed a lot of punishment carrying out the blitz—but that never was an issue.

"I enjoyed it," Wilson said. "It was a chance to get back at the quarterback. He stands around all day smiling at you."

When Wilson burst through, quarterbacks were not smiling.

KELLEN WINSLOW

Tight End
San Diego (1979-1987)

Ten seconds later, and the air might have gone out of Air Coryell.

San Diego coach Don Coryell already had top-flight receivers in Charlie Joiner and John Jefferson. He knew what he needed to flesh out his budding pass offense: Kellen Winslow, the multidimensional tight end from the University of Missouri. But the Chargers couldn't get Winslow where they were slotted in the first round of the 1979 draft. Finally, 10 seconds before Cleveland's time expired, the two teams worked a trade. San Diego moved up and quickly claimed Winslow.

The NFL rule book had been liberalized in 1978 and 1979 to generate more passing offense. Nobody took advantage of the new rules better than Winslow. No longer could tight ends be mobbed as they got off the line. When Winslow was left to run free, there wasn't a linebacker or strong safety in the league who could keep up with him. He was equipped with a tight end's body (6-5, 250) and a sprinter's speed.

He led the NFL in receiving in 1980 and 1981 (with 89 and 88 catches, respectively), and finished second with 54 in the strike-shortened 1982 season. He tied an NFL single-game record with 5 touchdown receptions against the Oakland Raiders in 1981.

If one game defines Winslow's NFL career, it was a 1981 AFC Divisional Playoff Game. Playing in humid conditions in Miami, the Chargers and Dolphins battled into overtime. Winslow caught 13 passes for 166 yards, and he blocked what could have been the winning kick at the end of regulation. The Chargers won 41-38 in overtime. Afterward, teammates had to help him from the field.

Only injuries could slow Winslow, who suffered a devastating knee injury in 1984. His arduous comeback resulted in several more productive years (and his fifth Pro Bowl selection), but he no longer was the unstoppable force he had been.

ROD WOODSON

Cornerback-Safety
Pittsburgh (1987-1996)
San Francisco (1997)
Baltimore (1998-present)

After a game against the Steelers in the early 1990s, Houston wide receiver Haywood Jeffires couldn't get cornerback Rod Woodson out of his brain. "He played cornerback, he played safety, he played linebacker," Jeffires lamented. "He covered, he blitzed, he did just about everything he wanted. I swear, he probably lined up at nose tackle, too."

An exaggeration? Sure. But there is no doubt that Woodson is multitalented. He was Pittsburgh's best punt and kickoff returner for several years. He even led the NFL with a kickoff-return average of 27.3 yards in 1989.

In his prime, Woodson was an athlete of improbable dimensions. A world-class hurdler at Purdue, he was one of the fastest men on the field every time he suited up.

"Rod's got the best physical makeup of anybody playing right now," former Steelers defensive coordinator Tony Dungy said in the early 1990s. "Size, speed, strength, quickness, ability to play the ball—he's got everything you need."

Woodson earned six Pro Bowl nods in his first eight seasons. He was NFL defensive player of the year in 1993 after intercepting 8 passes, forcing 2 fumbles, collecting 2 sacks, and blocking a field-goal attempt. He is a quick thinker and a superb tackler.

The idea that he is superhuman took a hit in 1995, when he suffered a torn knee ligament in the opener. He made an incredibly quick recovery and came back to play in Super Bowl XXX at the end of the season, but never fully regained his speed.

Undaunted, Woodson changed his game, relying on strength and savvy. The comeback came full circle in 1999, when he shared the league lead for most interceptions (7) and made the Pro Bowl as a free safety.

STEVE YOUNG

Quarterback
Tampa Bay (1985-86)
San Francisco (1987-present)

Of all the great college football players throughout the years, nobody was a bigger campus hero than Steve Young. Not only was he a great passer—he set an NCAA single-season record for completion percentage (71.3) as a senior—he also was a great-great-great grandson of Brigham Young, the beloved Mormon patriarch and the man for whom Steve's school was named.

For a while, it seemed to be all downhill from there.

Rather than playing in the NFL, Young opted for the Los Angeles Express of the USFL. He played two seasons with the Express, then signed with Tampa Bay in 1985 after the USFL folded. The Buccaneers, however, lacked talent. Young passed for 11 touchdowns and threw 21 interceptions in two seasons.

Even after coming to the 49ers in 1987, Young met with frustration. He spent most of his time holding a clipboard and backing up the great Joe Montana.

Young started only 10 games in four seasons, but he got his shot when Montana underwent elbow surgery in 1991. The left-handed quarterback was nothing short of remarkable, leading the NFL in passing three consecutive seasons. Still, questions lingered. Unlike Montana, Young had not taken the 49ers to a Super Bowl.

His image changed forever in 1994. He not only got San Francisco to Super Bowl XXIX, he also passed for a record 6 touchdowns in a 49-26 victory over San Diego. Grudgingly, 49ers fans came to accept the fun-loving athlete who used to tell his USFL center, "Snap the ball over my head, and let's see what happens."

There was a lot to like. Young threw every type of pass with an artist's touch, and his open-field running matched that of a halfback. In fact, he finished the 1999 season with more career rushing yards (4,239) than all but one quarterback (Randall Cunningham). And what of his passing numbers? Young is the NFL's all-time leader in passer rating.

All-Time NFL Team

Offense

QB	Johnny Unitas
RB	Jim Brown
RB	Walter Payton
WR	Don Hutson
WR	Jerry Rice
TE	John Mackey
T	Roosevelt Brown
T	Anthony Muñoz
G	John Hannah
G	Jim Parker
C	Mike Webster

DEFENSE

DE	DEACON JONES
DE	REGGIE WHITE
DT	JOE GREENE
DT	BOB LILLY
OLB	JACK HAM
OLB	LAWRENCE TAYLOR
MLB	DICK BUTKUS
CB	MEL BLOUNT
CB	NIGHT TRAIN LANE
S	RONNIE LOTT
S	LARRY WILSON

SPECIAL TEAMS

K	JAN STENERUD
KR	GALE SAYERS
P	RAY GUY
PR	DEION SANDERS
ST	STEVE TASKER

25
GREATEST
TEAMS
OF ALL TIME

GREEN BAY PACKERS 1929 © STILLER'S 1929 WORLD CHAMPIONS

The 1929 Packers had 28 players; 23 are pictured here.

1929
GREEN BAY PACKERS

In the haphazard era before the NFL Championship Game was established in 1933, the team that finished with the best won-lost record was awarded the league title. The Green Bay Packers had finished third in the standings in 1923 and second in 1927, and had not suffered a losing record in any of their first eight NFL seasons (1921-28).

But they didn't put it all together until 1929, when they won the first of what would become a record 12 titles. The addition of three players to the roster made all the difference.

Earl (Curly) Lambeau, who played one game at tailback in addition to his coaching and administrative duties, strengthened his club in the offseason by signing the free-spirited Johnny (Blood) McNally, a breakaway halfback; tackle Cal Hubbard, who, at 6 feet 5 inches and 250 pounds, was one of the NFL's largest players; and guard Mike Michalske, who dominated on both sides of the line. All of them, including Lambeau, were destined to earn spots in the Pro Football Hall of Fame.

The new roster additions quickly teamed with established Green Bay standouts—such as end LaVern Dilweg, fullback Bo Molenda, and tailback-punter Verne Lewellen—to form an imposing squad.

Not that the Packers had it easy. The New York Giants shadowed them all season. When the teams met at New York's Polo Grounds on November 24, Green Bay owned a record of 9-0, New York 8-0-1. The Packers won 20-6, using only 12 players.

That victory proved to be the difference in the standings. The Giants finished 13-1-1. The Packers tied the Frankford Yellow Jackets on Thanksgiving Day and ended the season with a record of 12-0-1, good enough for the top spot.

One indication of how clearly the Packers and Giants dominated the league is that only 1 of the league's other 10 teams (Frankford) ended the season with a winning record.

When the Packers returned home from Chicago after beating the Bears in the final game, a crowd of 20,000 surged onto the tracks and forced the team train to a halt.

The 1929 Packers fielded one of history's great defenses, allowing a mere 22 points in 13 games. They posted eight shutouts and yielded no more than 6 points to any team. Lambeau's squad repeated as champions in 1930 and 1931.

1936 GREEN BAY PACKERS

The seeds of the Packers' 1936 title were sown in 1933, when an NFL rule change opened up the passing game. Every team in the league had the opportunity to take advantage of the new system, but Green Bay coach Curly Lambeau was one step ahead of the pack.

Tailback Arnie Herber soon became the league's best passer. And when swift Don Hutson arrived from Alabama in 1935, the two became a nearly unstoppable combination.

The 1936 season was a signpost of stability for the NFL. No clubs were added or subtracted in the offseason, and for the first time, each team played the same number of games (12). On this level playing field, the Packers emerged as the dominant team.

They looked anything but supreme in the second week of the season, however, as the Bears beat them 30-3 at Green Bay's City Stadium. But the Packers regrouped, winning nine consecutive games to clinch the Western Division title. They ended the regular season with a scoreless tie against the Cardinals to finish with the league's best record (10-1-1).

Few of Green Bay's 10 victories were close. For the season, the team averaged nearly 21 points and gave up fewer than 10 per game. Herber led the league in passing (1,239 yards, 11 touchdowns), and Hutson scored 9 touchdowns and set an NFL record with 34 receptions.

In the title game, the stars lived up to their billing in a 21-6 victory over the Boston Redskins. Herber passed 48 yards to Hutson for one touchdown and set up another with a 52-yard pass to veteran halfback Johnny (Blood) McNally. Fullback Clarke Hinkle set up the final touchdown when he recovered a blocked punt at the Redskins' 3-yard line.

The Packers limited Boston to 130 yards in the 1936 title game.

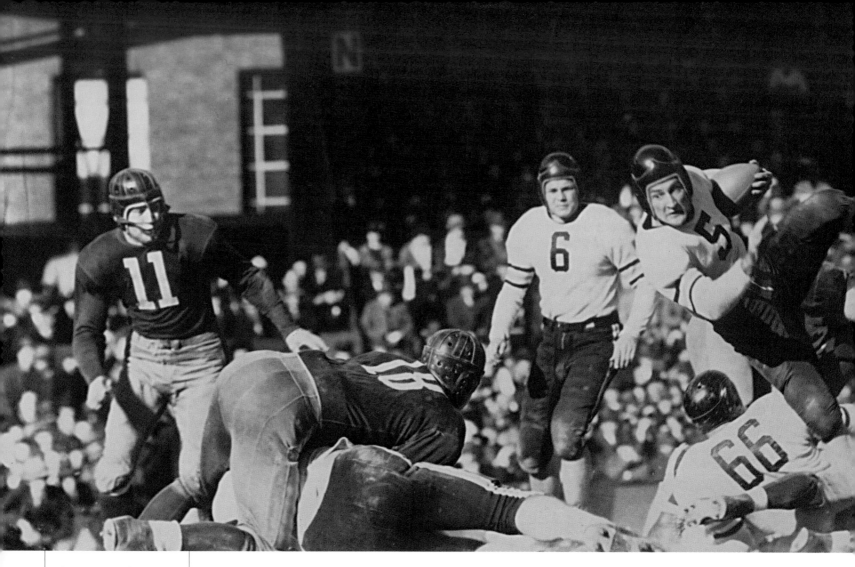

1940
CHICAGO BEARS

The T-formation, once viewed as a turn-of-the-century dinosaur good only for power running, enjoyed a rebirth during the 1930s. Tinkering by the Bears, who had never given up on the system, produced a modern T-formation from which teams could run or pass. The modern T, which also utilized a man in motion, helped the Bears win titles in 1932 and 1933.

The system really began to click in 1939, when Chicago drafted Sid Luckman, a former tailback from Columbia. Even as a rookie, Luckman proved masterful in the T, and he led the team to an 8-3 record and second place in the Western Division.

Luckman was surrounded by talent. The line was set with George Musso, Dan Fortmann (both guards, though Musso outweighed his partner by 63 pounds), and tackle Joe Stydahar. The 1940 draft brought standout center Clyde (Bulldog) Turner, and the Bears traded for

George (One-Play) McAfee, the Philadelphia Eagles' first-round draft pick. McAfee ran 93 yards for a touchdown against Green Bay with the first kickoff he fielded. That quick-strike ability earned McAfee his nickname.

Chicago, propelled by the league's top rushing attack, roared to a 6-1 start in 1940, then came back to the pack with narrow losses to Detroit (17-14) and Washington (7-3). The Bears regrouped to beat the Rams (47-25) and Cardinals (31-23) in their final two games to finish 8-3 and win the Western Division.

That set up a showdown with Washington in the 1940 NFL Championship Game. The Redskins had foiled the Bears' T in the first meeting, but George Halas, the Bears' owner and coach, had some help this time. Halas brought in Stanford coach Clark Shaughnessy, a noted expert on the T, to tune up the game plan.

The result was unlike anything seen before or since on an NFL field. Chicago overwhelmed Washington in every phase to produce the biggest blowout (73-0) and one of the most stunning results in the history of pro sports.

What soon followed came as no surprise: The T became the NFL's basic formation.

And yet the Bears could not shake Green Bay, which was fueled by the prolific passing combination of quarterback Cecil Isbell and end Don Hutson. The Bears beat the Packers 25-17 on opening day; the Packers returned the favor 16-14 on November 2.

By the end of the regular season, the two rivals found themselves tied atop the Western Division at 10-1, producing the first divisional playoff game in NFL history. Playing one week after the bombing of Pearl Harbor, Chicago broke free for 24 second-quarter points and coasted to a 33-14 victory.

A week later, the Bears faced the Giants for the championship at chilly Wrigley Field. Despite controlling the ball for 53 of 63 plays in the first half, Chicago led only 9-6, earning the players a halftime rebuke from George Halas. "You people are supposed to be champions," said Halas, the club's owner and coach, "but you're playing like bums."

They got the message. In the second half, Luckman led the Bears on touchdown drives of 71, 66, and 54 yards, and Ken Kavanaugh returned a fumble 42 yards for a touchdown in a 37-9 victory. Chicago became the first team to win consecutive NFL Championship Games.

The Bears celebrated after their second title-game rout.

1941
CHICAGO BEARS

The 1941 Chicago Bears did not run up an outrageous score in the championship game. From beginning to end, however, they probably were superior to the 1940 squad.

A talent-saturated roster got even better with the drafting of fullback Norm Standlee and halfback Hugh Gallarneau from Stanford's Rose Bowl team. They alternated with Bill Osmanski and George McAfee in an impressive backfield, helping Chicago lead the NFL in both rushing and passing. McAfee averaged a league-leading 7.3 yards per carry, and quarterback Sid Luckman completed a league-leading 57.1 percent of his passes.

This was one of pro football's first great offensive teams. In one three-week stretch in October, the Bears outscored the Rams 48-21, the Cardinals 53-7, and the Lions 49-0. Overall, the Bears outscored opponents 396-147 for an average per-game score of 36-13.

1949
Philadelphia
Eagles

Steve Van Buren ran for a record 196 yards against the Rams.

In the late 1940s, the Philadelphia Eagles were the class of the NFL.

The Eagles were led by coach Earle (Greasy) Neale, who declared that he would rather lose 100-99 than win 3-0. Despite his offensive slant, Neale still built an innovative and aggressive defense called the Eagle in which Philadelphia showed the then-standard seven-man front before dropping the ends into pass coverage.

The Eagles were potent on offense, too, with quarterback Tommy Thompson and end Pete Pihos, who excelled as both a pass receiver and a defender. Mostly, though, the Eagles had Steve Van Buren, a runner with the speed of a sprinter and the temperament of a pit bull.

Philadelphia met the Chicago Cardinals in consecutive NFL title games, losing in 1947 and winning in 1948. The team was sold in 1949, to a group of 100 investors who paid $3,000 each. The new owners were rewarded with a nearly unbeatable team.

The Eagles' only blemish in 1949 was a 38-21 loss to the Bears on October 16. After that, nobody came within 14 points of Neale's team.

Their most impressive victory was a 38-14 romp over the previously unbeaten Rams on November 6. Philadelphia scored more than 40 points three times and recorded two shutouts. For the season, the 11-1 Eagles outscored their opponents 364-134.

Van Buren set an NFL record with 1,146 rushing yards, and fellow halfback Bosh Pritchard led the league with an average of 6.0 yards per carry. Thompson was the league's third-ranked passer. The Eagles even boasted talent in their rookie class with center-linebacker Chuck Bednarik.

Playing at home, the Eagles had won the 1948 championship in a blinding snowstorm. In 1949, the title game was in Los Angeles, home of the Western Division champion Rams, who anticipated dry turf and solid footing. Instead, a deluge dumped two inches of rain on the Los Angeles Coliseum the day before the game, and the teams spent the afternoon slogging through a quagmire.

The mud bothered just about everyone on the field except Van Buren. He carried 31 times for 196 yards to propel Philadelphia to a 14-0 victory, its second successive title-game shutout.

1950
CLEVELAND BROWNS

The Cleveland Browns dominated the All-America Football Conference from 1946-49, the only four years of that league's existence. But when the AAFC's Browns, 49ers, and Colts joined the NFL in 1950, few gave the Browns hope of continuing that supremacy in the more established league.

A closer look would have revealed that the Browns were no fluke, a championship team comprised of players handpicked by legendary coach Paul Brown. Otto Graham, one of pro football's greatest quarterbacks, ran the show. He had Marion Motley at fullback, Dante Lavelli and Mac Speedie at ends, and the versatile (halfback-wingback-tailback) Dub Jones everywhere else. Cleveland also picked up Len Ford, a talented end who had played with the AAFC's Los Angeles Dons.

Still, NFL fans grinned when the 1950 schedule had Cleveland visiting the defending-champion Eagles in the first week. Predictably, the game turned into a rout. Unexpectedly, the Eagles were the victims, enduring a stunning 35-10 defeat as Graham passed for 346 yards.

The victory vindicated the Browns and their coach, who later proved he could alter his game plan to fit the situation. After the game against the Eagles, NFL loyalists derided the Browns as a one-dimensional team that had to pass to win. Brown remembered, and when the teams met in a rematch that Cleveland had to win to stay alive, the Browns did not attempt a single pass while beating the Eagles 13-7.

Cleveland's one stumbling block was the New York Giants, who threw their Umbrella defense at Brown's offense and came away with two low-scoring victories. Cleveland and New York tied for the division lead at 10-2.

The third time was a charm for the Browns, who outlasted New York 8-3 in an icy, windy playoff game along Lake Erie. A week later, they edged the Rams for the NFL championship.

NUMBER 60 OR 14?
When the Cleveland Browns honored Otto Graham by retiring his jersey number, it was number 14 that they removed from use. But earlier in his career, fans knew him as number 60.

1958
BALTIMORE COLTS

If the Baltimore Colts of the late 1950s displayed remarkable resilience, perhaps it was because so many of them had come from the scrap heap.

Quarterback Johnny Unitas had played for a semipro team after the Steelers cut him in 1955. His favorite target, less-than-speedy end Raymond Berry, was a twentieth-round choice in 1954. The team's dominant defensive linemen, tackle Art Donovan and end Gino Marchetti, had played for the 1952 Dallas Texans, the last NFL team to fold. All four players would earn spots in the Pro Football Hall of Fame, along with two other teammates, halfback Lenny Moore and offensive tackle Jim Parker.

Under head coach Weeb Ewbank, the ragamuffins came together to form an imposing team in 1958. The Colts won their first six games, capping the streak with a 56-0 massacre of Green Bay. Two weeks later, they defeated the Bears 17-0, the first time Chicago had been shut out in 146 games.

The Colts lost only three games, once when Unitas was forced to sit out with a punctured lung, and twice after they had clinched the Western Conference championship. To win the NFL title, though, Baltimore had to travel to Yankee Stadium and face the Giants, who had just shut down the great Jim Brown and the Cleveland Browns in a playoff game.

The 1958 NFL Championship Game often is described as the greatest game ever played. The seesaw battle between the Colts and Giants held a national television audience spellbound. It took a miraculous drive, with Unitas hitting Berry time and again, to position the Colts for a tying field goal that forced the first overtime in NFL history. Unitas moved the Colts again in the extra period, and fullback Alan Ameche's 1-yard touchdown plunge secured a place in history for his team.

1960
PHILADELPHIA
EAGLES

In 1958, the Philadelphia Eagles were 2-9-1. By 1962, they were 3-10-1. Halfway in between, they experienced a fairy-tale season.

The 1960 Eagles had a number of good players, but most agree they would have gone nowhere without a pair of graybeards: Norm Van Brocklin and Chuck Bednarik. Van Brocklin, the fiery quarterback who set records with the Rams, was 34 years old and playing in his final season. He made it a memorable one, passing for 2,471 yards and 24 touchdowns.

Bednarik was 35. Once a two-way star, he settled in at center for Philadelphia. But when injuries depleted the defense, he also played linebacker and became the "Last of the 60-Minute Men." Bednarik averaged 58 minutes per game for most of the season.

The Eagles got off to a lethargic start in 1960. They lost their home opener 41-24 to the Browns, then barely got by Dallas, an expansion team. But then the Eagles won eight games in a row. The key victory was a 31-29 nail-biter over Cleveland in which Bobby Walston kicked a 39-yard field goal with two seconds left.

The Eagles had no running game. (Only the Cowboys rushed for fewer yards.) So Van Brocklin went to the air with abandon, making use of his outstanding trio of receivers, ends Walston and Pete Retzlaff and flanker Tommy McDonald. Philadelphia finished 10-2 and won the Eastern Conference championship.

The title game was appropriately dramatic. After Green Bay took a 13-10 lead, Van Brocklin led the Eagles to a go-ahead touchdown with 5:21 left. The game ended at the Eagles' 8-yard line, where Bednarik tackled Jim Taylor as time expired. The outcome marked Green Bay coach Vince Lombardi's only postseason loss.

MODERN BANKING
After pulling two-way duty during the 1960 season, Chuck Bednarik figured he deserved a raise. The Eagles agreed, signing him to a $20,000 contract for 1961. Bednarik then took his check home and did what he always did—shoved it in a sock. The Eagles eventually had to call Bednarik and ask him to cash his checks so they could keep their books straight.

Chuck Bednarik (60) wrapped up the 1960 title for the Eagles.

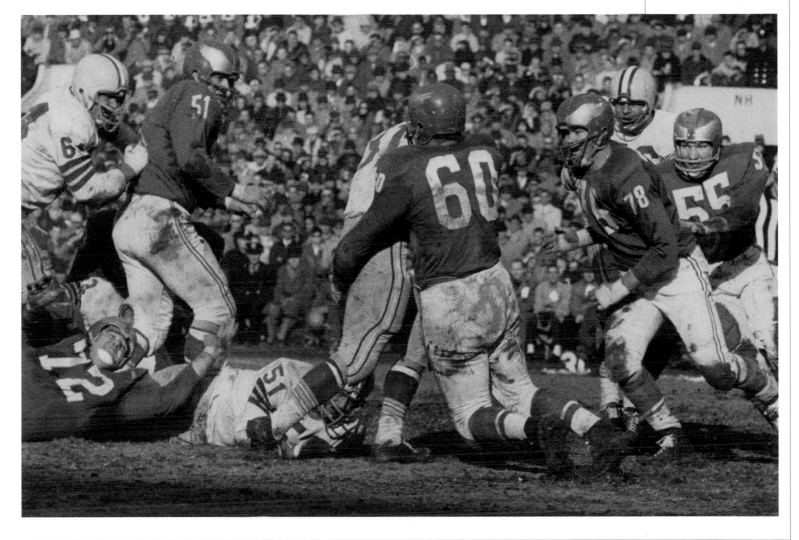

1962
GREEN BAY PACKERS

Jim Taylor (31) bulled his way to 85 yards in the 1962 title game.

Upon hiring Vince Lombardi as head coach in 1959, the Green Bay Packers immediately began an upward trajectory. A team that had not posted a winning record in a dozen years went 7-5 in 1959, 8-4 in 1960 (followed by a loss to the Eagles in the NFL Championship Game), and 11-3 in 1961 (followed by a victory over the Giants in the title game).

The best was yet to come.

Most of Lombardi's roster consisted of holdovers, with a handful of additions. He had Bart Starr at quarterback, Jim Taylor at fullback, and Paul Hornung at halfback. He had an inpenetrable offensive line anchored by tackle Forrest Gregg. He had a disciplined defense paced by end Willie Davis, middle linebacker Ray Nitschke, and cornerback Herb Adderley.

Even the loss of Hornung for five games with injuries didn't slow the Packers.

The Packers jumped to a 10-0 start, with only two of the victories by fewer than 11 points. They routed the Bears and the Eagles, each by the score of 49-0. Only the Lions, who sacked Bart Starr 11 times in a Thanksgiving Day upset, rained on their 13-1 parade.

Taylor was the soul of the 1962 team. The burly runner had his best season, setting an NFL record with 19 touchdowns and leading the league with 1,474 rushing yards. It was the only time in Jim Brown's career that the Cleveland legend failed to win the rushing title. Starr was the NFL's leading passer, and safety Willie Wood intercepted a league-high 9 passes.

Green Bay slugged it out with the Giants again in the 1962 NFL Championship Game. Taylor accounted for most of the offense, with 31 carries for 85 tough yards, but the Packers' defense carried the day in a 16-7 victory. New York failed to score on offense, its only touchdown coming on a blocked punt.

1963
CHICAGO BEARS

Scanning their respective rosters, it is hard to imagine that George Halas's Chicago Bears could outclass Lombardi's Packers in 1963. But with a new zone pass-coverage system installed by assistant coach George Allen, Chicago found a potent weapon in its defense.

Defensive ends Doug Atkins and Ed O'Bradovich supplied the pass rush, linebackers Bill George and Larry Morris blanketed the short pass patterns, and the Bears led the NFL in a variety of defensive statistical categories—fewest points allowed (144, just 10.3 per game), fewest yards allowed (226.9 per game), and most interceptions (36).

The offense was not explosive, but it was reliable. Bill Wade, who directed the attack, passed for 2,301 yards. His favorite receiver was young tight end Mike Ditka, who made 59 receptions. The Bears suffered only 25 turnovers, while the defense forced 54.

The emphasis on defense often produced low-scoring victories—10-3 at Green Bay on opening day; 10-3 over Baltimore; 6-0 over Los Angeles. The Bears held or shared first place all season, but the Packers never were far behind.

The key to the season was a November 17 rematch at Wrigley Field in which Chicago waltzed past Green Bay 26-7. Though the Bears tied their next two games (against Pittsburgh and Minnesota), they won their last two to finish 11-1-2, a half-game ahead of the Packers in the Western Conference.

The 1963 title game was a perfect showcase for the snarling Bears. Wade completed only 10 of 28 passes in 8-degree weather, while the Giants' Y.A. Tittle completed just 11 of 29. The difference was turnovers. Chicago intercepted Tittle 5 times, and 2 of the thefts (by Morris and O'Bradovich) set up touchdown runs by Wade. Chicago won 14-10 for its first title in 17 years.

The right arm of Bill Wade (9) supplied most of the Bears' offense in 1963.

THE LAST HURRAH
The NFL championship won by the Chicago Bears in 1963 was the club's eighth title, a record at the time. The Bears won six of those championships with their founder and owner, George Halas, prowling the sideline as coach, including 1963, which was his final title.

1966
GREEN BAY PACKERS

PACKERS OF FAME
The 1966 Green Bay Packers featured nine players destined for the Pro Football Hall of Fame: Herb Adderley, Willie Davis, Forrest Gregg, Paul Hornung, Henry Jordan, Ray Nitschke, Bart Starr, Jim Taylor, and Willie Wood. Coach Vince Lombardi preceded them, inducted posthumously in 1971.

Vince Lombardi's Packers played in three consecutive NFL Championship Games from 1960-62 and, after a short hiatus, were back for three more from 1965-67.

The roster underwent a few changes between those runs. Kicker-punter Don Chandler arrived in 1965, as did flanker Carroll Dale. Dave Robinson was elevated to a starting spot at outside linebacker, and halfback Donny Anderson showed up in 1966. But Green Bay relied on the same nucleus throughout the regime, and the team was at its peak in 1966.

Jim Taylor spearheaded the Packers' ground attack with 705 yards. Bart Starr led the NFL in passing, completing 62.2 percent of his attempts and throwing only 3 interceptions. The defense played at its highest level, yielding just 163 points during the regular season and holding seven teams to 10 points or fewer. Green Bay won its final five games to finish 12-2, the two losses coming by a total of four points.

There was an extra intensity to the 1966 season. The AFL-NFL merger agreement had been finalized in the offseason, and one offshoot was a showdown between the champions of both leagues. Lombardi's troops were under tremendous pressure to uphold the old order.

First, the Packers had to defeat the suddenly formidable Cowboys in the NFL title game. The game came down to the wire. With Dallas at Green Bay's 2-yard line in the final minute, the Packers' Tom Brown intercepted a pass by Don Meredith in the end zone.

The first AFL-NFL World Championship Game—not yet officially dubbed the Super Bowl—was historic, but not nearly as thrilling. The Packers turned a 14-10 halftime lead into a 35-10 walkover, preserving NFL dominance for the time being. The Packers would return one year later and defeat Oakland in Super Bowl II.

1968
NEW YORK JETS

As the 1968 season progressed, football fans heaped praise on the Baltimore Colts of the NFL, who were on their way to a sterling 13-1 record. The New York Jets were making noise in the AFL, but that league had yet to be taken seriously by NFL standard-bearers.

The Jets were armed with the AFL's most celebrated player, quarterback Joe Namath (number 12, below), who in 1967 became the first man to pass for more than 4,000 yards in a season. Namath passed for 3,147 in 1968, despite undergoing surgery to his left knee during the offseason. New York also had a strong backfield duo in Matt Snell and Emerson Boozer, part of an offense that scored 419 points.

The Jets, who never were really challenged in the Eastern Division, won several close games and finished 11-3. Even when they lost, it was interesting. In the "Heidi Game," New York led Oakland 32-29 with 1:05 to play on November 17, only to give up 2 touchdowns and lose 43-32 (the end of the game's telecast was pre-empted by the start of the movie *Heidi*.)

The Jets got another shot at the Raiders in the AFL title game, and they made the most of it. Namath passed for 3 touchdowns to build a 27-23 lead, and the Jets preserved the victory in the final minutes by recovering an errant lateral the Raiders assumed to be an incomplete pass.

Then came the day of reckoning against the Colts, who were favored by 18 to 21 points in Super Bowl III. Namath made news when he "guaranteed" a victory. He backed up his words, calling a masterful game at the line of scrimmage and leading the Jets to a stunning 16-7 triumph.

The victory not only made a folk legend of Namath and pro football champions of the Jets, it also put the AFL on equal footing with the established league.

The quick release and savvy play-calling of Joe Namath (12) kept the Colts at bay.

1972
MIAMI DOLPHINS

Just six years after they played their first game as an AFL expansion team, coach Don Shula's Miami Dolphins did something unmatched, either before or after the 1972 season: They won every game, all 17 they played.

To be sure, they occasionally escaped defeat by the skin of their teeth. In the third game of the season, Garo Yepremian kicked a 51-yard field goal and quarterback Bob Griese tossed a 3-yard touchdown pass with 1:28 remaining to rally the Dolphins to a 16-14 victory over the Vikings in Minnesota. Three weeks later, Yepremian's 54-yard field goal helped Miami defeat Buffalo 24-23 in the Orange Bowl.

Between those two games, the Dolphins' season took a peculiar twist. Griese, the canny field leader, was sidelined by a broken leg and a dislocated ankle when hit by San Diego's Ron East. He watched most of the rest of the season from a distance as 38-year-old Earl Morrall, Miami's unlikely backup quarterback, took command of the team.

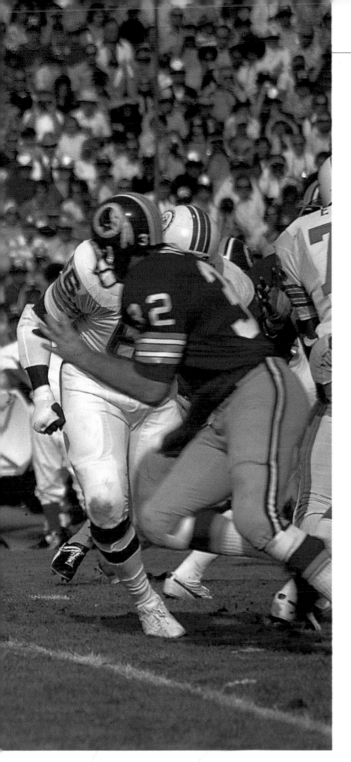

and safeties Dick Anderson and Jake Scott made life miserable for ball carriers. The No-Name Defense posted two shutouts against Shula's former team, the Baltimore Colts, as well as a 52-0 drubbing of the New England Patriots.

Expectations mounted alongside victories as the season wore on, but the Dolphins didn't crack, not even in a pair of close playoff games. It took an 8-yard touchdown run in the fourth quarter by backup running back Jim Kiick to defeat Cleveland 20-14 on Christmas Eve.

A week later, Miami traveled to Pittsburgh to play the Steelers for the AFC crown (at that time, home sites for conference title games were rotated rather than awarded to the team with the best record). The Dolphins trailed 7-0 until punter Larry Seiple, to the surprise of everyone (including his coach), took off running on fourth-and-5 from the Steelers' 49. His 37-yard run set up the tying touchdown. After Pittsburgh took a 10-7 third-quarter lead, Griese returned to action for the first time in three months and rallied Miami to a 21-17 victory.

Amazingly, the undefeated Dolphins were slight underdogs to the Washington Redskins in Super Bowl VII. But the Dolphins, as they had all season, came out on top. Miami's swarming defense intercepted 3 of quarterback Billy Kilmer's passes, and Csonka ran for 112 yards. Only a touchdown return on a botched field-goal attempt—which Yepremian tried to pass, in comic fashion—kept Washington from being shut out.

A workmanlike 14-7 victory was enough to guarantee the 17-0 Dolphins an unprecedented place in NFL lore.

LASTING IMAGE
Don Shula, whose image is featured on the coin commemorating Super Bowl VII, left his own calling card in the NFL record books: a won-lost record of 347-173-6.

A perfect ending: Don Shula goes for a ride after Super Bowl VII.

Fortunately for Morrall, he could rely on an unrelenting ground attack to handle the lion's share of the load. The 1972 Dolphins became the first team to produce two 1,000-yard runners in the same season: human wrecking-ball fullback Larry Csonka and speedy halfback Eugene (Mercury) Morris. As a team, the Dolphins rushed for an NFL-record 2,960 yards.

On the other side of the ball, a well-drilled, if starless, collection of tacklers consistently shut down opponents. The No-Name Defense, as it was affectionately called, was especially tough up the middle, where defensive tackle Manny Fernandez, middle linebacker Nick Buoniconti,

1973
MIAMI DOLPHINS

Ball carriers found few avenues against the No-Name Defense.

The most intriguing question of the 1973 NFL season—whether the Miami Dolphins could again go undefeated—was answered rather hastily by the Raiders, who scored a 12-7 victory in week two. Undaunted, the Dolphins reeled off 10 consecutive victories to claim their third consecutive AFC East title.

Coach Don Shula's recipe for success—ball control and ubiquitous defense—basically was unchanged from the preceding year. Running behind a trio of talented blockers—center Jim Langer and guards Larry Little and Bob Kuechenberg—Larry Csonka finished second in the AFC with 1,003 yards, while Mercury Morris averaged 6.4 yards per carry. Coordinator Bill Arnsparger's 53 Defense, named for the jersey number of "swingman" Bob Matheson, held 11

opponents to 14 points or less. Included were shutouts of the Colts (44-0) and Bills (17-0).

Miami seemed to find a different way to win each week. Against the Colts, defensive back Tim Foley returned 2 blocked punts for touchdowns, an NFL first. Against Detroit, wide receiver Paul Warfield caught 4 scoring passes from Bob Griese en route to a 34-7 victory.

The postseason was a happy romp for the Dolphins. They collared Cincinnati 34-16, then used 266 rushing yards to dominate Oakland 27-10 in the AFC Championship Game. Super Bowl VIII never was in doubt. Miami scored 14 points in the first quarter on the way to a 24-7 victory over the overmatched Vikings. Griese, the model of bland efficiency, attempted only 7 passes and completed 6. Csonka chugged for 145 yards and 2 touchdowns on 33 carries.

The Dolphins won their fourth consecutive division title in 1974, but lost in the playoffs. In 1975, Csonka, Warfield, and running back Jim Kiick left for the World Football League, signaling the end of Miami's reign.

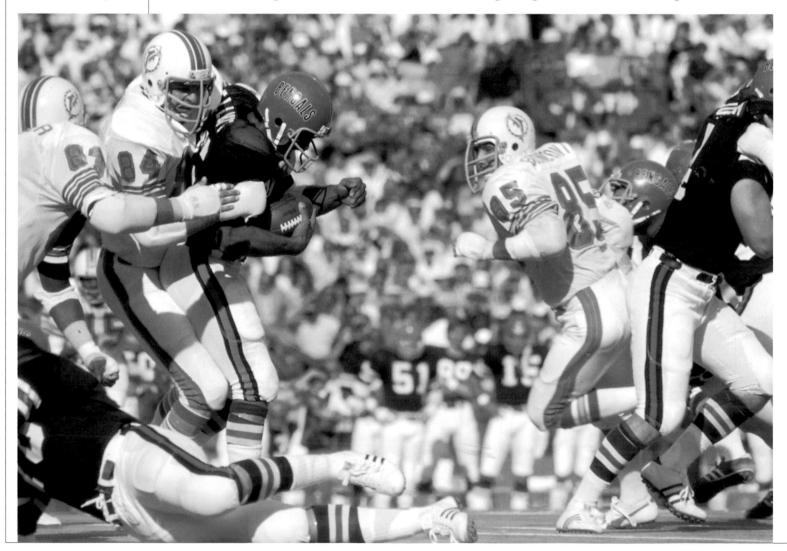

1975 PITTSBURGH STEELERS

For nearly the first 40 years of their existence, the Pittsburgh Steelers (originally called the Pirates) were the whipping boys of the NFL. From 1933 to 1971, they participated in exactly one postseason game—a 21-0 loss to the Philadelphia Eagles in 1947.

Benevolent owner Art Rooney stuck with the team, and so, for the most part, did the fans of Pittsburgh. Their patience was rewarded in 1972, when the Steelers made the first of eight consecutive playoff appearances. They won Super Bowl IX after the 1974 season, and by 1975 they were in full bloom.

Though Pittsburgh had substantial offensive firepower in 1975, the team's strength was its defense. Cornerback Mel Blount intercepted 11 passes and was named NFL defensive player of the year. Defensive tackle Mean Joe Greene and linebackers Jack Lambert and Jack Ham were at the pinnacle of their careers.

After a surprising home loss to Buffalo in the second week of the season, the "Steel Curtain" defense came to life. The next three marks in the victory ledger were by scores of 42-6 at Cleveland, 20-9 over Denver, and 34-3 over Chicago. The Steelers did not lose again until the final week of the regular season.

The Steel Curtain was at its best in Pittsburgh's first playoff game. It sacked the Colts' quarterbacks 5 times, forced 4 turnovers, and held Baltimore to 154 total yards in a 28-10 victory. A week later, the Steelers defeated Oakland 16-10 in 16-degree weather at Three Rivers Stadium, the clock expiring with the Raiders at Pittsburgh's 15-yard line.

The final showdown, against the Dallas Cowboys, was Super Bowl X in Miami. The Curtain came down again, sacking quarterback Roger Staubach 7 times and forcing him into 3 interceptions in a 21-17 victory. Lynn Swann caught 4 passes for 161 yards in a gracefully spectacular performance, and Steel City was football's capital.

Terry Bradshaw (12) posted his best passer rating (88.0) in 1975.

GRACEFUL SWANN
Lynn Swann put on a clinic in Super Bowl X. His juggling 53-yard catch (above) is regarded as one of the greatest ever, and he also had a 64-yard touchdown that proved decisive. He was named the game's MVP.

1976
OAKLAND RAIDERS

The Oakland Raiders of the Richard Nixon era were viewed as the second-best team in football, no matter who was number one. They lost six AFL or AFC Championship Games between 1968-1975, and the team that defeated them went on to win the Super Bowl every time. But second place simply wasn't good enough for driven owner Al Davis or emotional head coach John Madden.

In 1976, the Raiders made up for missed opportunities of the past.

Strangely, the turning point was a 48-17 blowout loss at the hands of the New England Patriots in week 4. After New England took advantage of the Raiders' injury-ravaged defense, Madden decided it was time to forgo his traditional 4-3 defense and switch to a 3-4 alignment. The revamped defense excelled as the team won its last 10 games.

There never was any question about the offense. Quarterback Ken Stabler completed two-thirds of his passes and fired 27 touchdown passes. His multiple weapons included the hands of Fred Biletnikoff, the speed of Cliff Branch, and the brawn of tight end Dave Casper. Fullback Mark van Eeghen and halfback Clarence Davis were a solid one-two punch.

In a divisional playoff game, the Raiders got a scare from their new nemesis, New England. They needed 2 fourth-quarter touchdowns, the last a bootleg by the brittle-kneed Stabler with 10 seconds left, to secure a 24-21 victory. The subsequent showdown with the Steelers lost its buzz as Pittsburgh's starting running backs sat out with injuries; Oakland won easily 24-7.

The Raiders were brilliant in a 32-14 victory in Super Bowl XI. The left side of the offensive line—guard Gene Upshaw and tackle Art Shell—manhandled Minnesota's Alan Page and Jim Marshall en route to a record 266 rushing yards. Madden left the field riding atop his players' shoulders.

"I always felt, and I still feel to this day, that the toughest part is getting to the Super Bowl," Shell said. "Once you got there, it was easy because we knew how to win."

Protected by a formidable offensive line, Ken Stabler (12) finished 1976 as the NFL's top passer.

1977
DALLAS COWBOYS

The Dallas Cowboys had been one of the dominant teams of the 1970s, claiming four division titles and six playoff spots between 1970 and 1976. But they had not won the Super Bowl since the 1971 season. So, shortly before the 1977 draft, the Cowboys shipped four draft choices to Seattle for the second overall pick, which they used to select running back Tony Dorsett, the Heisman Trophy winner from the University of Pittsburgh. Dallas envisioned Dorsett as the final piece of the puzzle, and he turned out to be precisely that.

Dorsett started only four regular-season games, but the speedster still managed to run for 1,007 yards and 12 touchdowns. His legs were the perfect complement to the arm of Roger Staubach, who, at 35, was the NFC's highest-rated quarterback. Staubach's favorite targets were wide receiver Drew Pearson, who had 48 receptions, and running back Preston Pearson (no relation), who had 46.

Dallas won the first eight games on its schedule, then lost to the Cardinals and Steelers in back-to-back weeks. That proved to be a short-lived skid, as the Cowboys bounced back to win four successive games and finish 12-2, tied with the Denver Broncos for the best record in the NFL.

In the postseason, Dallas's talented defense took center stage. Head coach Tom Landry had perfected his Flex II system, and it peaked at the right time. In the divisional playoffs, safety Charlie Waters intercepted 3 passes in a 37-6 rout of Chicago. The next round brought a 23-6 victory over Minnesota in which the Cowboys limited the Vikings to 66 rushing yards.

Super Bowl XII, contested at the New Orleans Superdome, was the first played indoors, and there was nowhere for the Broncos to hide. Dallas intercepted 4 passes, collected 4 sacks, and recovered 4 fumbles. Denver replaced starting quarterback Craig Morton, who formerly played for the Cowboys, with Norris Weese, but neither could find a way to generate any offense.

The Broncos finished the game with a paltry 35 passing yards as the Cowboys coasted to a 27-10 triumph.

Tony Dorsett (33) took the heat off Roger Staubach (12).

DOOMSDAY REDUX
The Dallas offense received the headlines in 1977, but the so-called Doomsday II Defense (Doomsday I keyed the club's victory in Super Bowl VI) was equally potent. In fact, the stars of Super Bowl XII were defensive linemen Harvey Martin (above) and Randy White, who shared MVP honors.

1978 PITTSBURGH STEELERS

Just when you thought it was safe to step foot on an NFL field, the Steelers were back.

There had been a few subtractions (such as linebacker Andy Russell, who retired, and defensive tackle Ernie Holmes, who was traded after the 1977 season) and a few additions to the starting lineup (such as hard-hitting safety Donnie Shell and center Mike Webster) since their last Super Bowl victory. In large part, though, these were the same Steelers who had thrashed the competition in 1974-75.

Actually, they probably were better. The defense, though older, seemed as mighty as ever. Pittsburgh held eight opponents to 10 points or less, allowing the fewest points in the league (195 in the first 16-game season). Meanwhile, the offense had become better balanced. Running back Franco Harris posted his standard 1,000-yard season, and quarterback Terry Bradshaw came into his own, leading the NFL with 28 touchdown passes.

The Steelers were 7-0 before they hit a road bump, a 24-17 loss to Houston and rookie Earl Campbell. They entered the playoffs with a 14-2 record and a five-game winning streak. The new-look Steelers then showed their explosive side. Bradshaw fired 2 long scoring passes in a 44-second span of the fourth quarter to beat Denver 33-10. A week later, they encountered little resistance in a 34-5 victory over the Oilers.

The familiar, scowling faces of the Cowboys awaited in Super Bowl XIII. The two NFL heavyweights put on a show. Pittsburgh built a 35-17 lead behind Bradshaw, who passed for 318 yards and 4 touchdowns (2 to wide receiver John Stallworth, the team's newest star), then held on for a 35-31 victory. The Steelers would repeat in Super Bowl XIV.

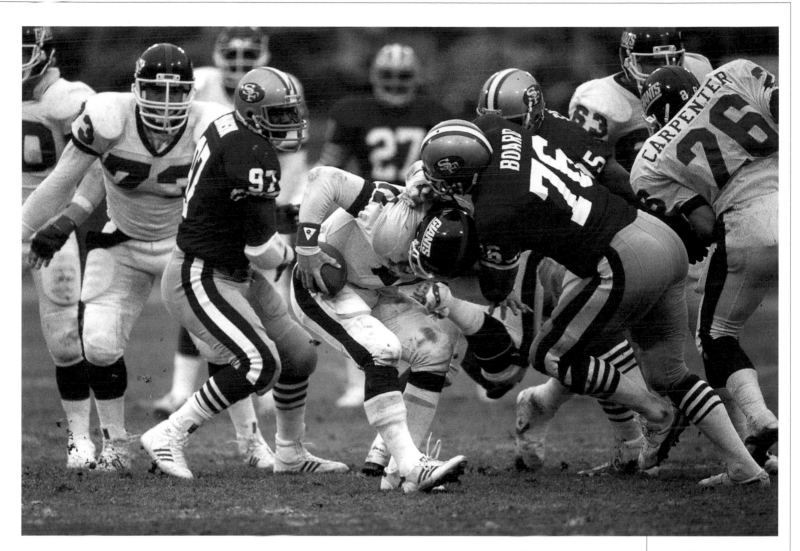

1984
SAN FRANCISCO
49ERS

The San Francisco 49ers won their first Super Bowl after the 1981 season, but it seemed more an aberration than a sign of things to come. A year later, in the strike-shortened 1982 season, they missed the playoffs.

By 1984, the smoke cleared to reveal a lineup virtually without weakness. The 49ers were the first NFL team to win 15 games in a regular season. Their only loss was 20-17 to Pittsburgh, on Gary Anderson's field goal with less than two minutes left. They swept the second-place Rams in the NFC West with a 33-0 blowout on the road and a 19-16 verdict to end the season.

San Francisco scored 475 points, an average of nearly 30 per game, while the defense— sparked by cornerbacks Ronnie Lott and Eric Wright—allowed fewer points (227) than any other team in the league. Quarterback Joe Montana led the NFC in passing, running back Wendell Tyler set a club rushing record with 1,262 yards, and kicker Ray Wersching led the NFL with 131 points.

The 49ers got defensive in the playoffs. After allowing the Giants 10 first-half points in a divisional playoff game, they didn't surrender another score for six quarters as they dispatched New York 21-10 and the Bears 23-0.

As Super Bowl XIX approached, most of the attention went to the AFC-champion Dolphins and Dan Marino. The electrifying second-year quarterback had shredded the NFL record book with 5,084 passing yards and 48 touchdowns during the regular season. But San Francisco struck a blow for balance.

Coach Bill Walsh of the 49ers deployed six defensive backs, and the scheme limited Marino's ability to stretch the field. Montana passed for 331 yards and ran for 59, and running back Roger Craig scored 3 touchdowns in the 49ers' convincing 38-16 victory.

The 49ers' defense dominated opponents in the 1984 playoffs.

SOMETHING TO PROVE
After the 49ers defeated the Dolphins in Super Bowl XIX, they admitted that they went into the game with a chip on their shoulders. Center Randy Cross explained: "We were seventeen-and-one and people were asking us, 'Gee, do you really think you can stay with the Dolphins?' It was like a slap in the face. We had something to prove in that game. I don't want to say we hated the Dolphins by the end of the week, but...."

1985
CHICAGO BEARS

SWEETNESS
The 1985 Bears weren't only about defense. Their backfield included the NFL's all-time rushing leader, Walter (Sweetness) Payton. The nickname referred to both his graceful playing style and his demeanor.

The Bears' blitz made offenses frantic and footballs fly in 1985.

They weren't able to sustain their success long enough to earn the "dynasty" tag, but for one scintillating year, the Chicago Bears may have been the best football team ever.

Mike Ditka's ball-control game plan revolved around Walter Payton. The immortal running back was 31 by the start of the season, but he was spry enough to rush for 1,551 yards. Jim McMahon, the punk-rock quarterback, had a career-best 2,392 passing yards.

It was more than enough to get by, thanks to the fearsome defensive squad fielded by coordinator Buddy Ryan. After a few years of tinkering, Ryan perfected an aggressive, blitzing scheme dubbed the "46 Defense."

The 1985 Bears led the league in fewest points (12.4) and yards (258.4) allowed per game. Their secondary was little more than average. But they had solid run-stuffers up front, including tackles Dan Hampton and William (Refrigerator) Perry. Middle linebacker Mike Singletary might have been the best player in football in 1985. A trio of quick pass rushers, end Richard Dent and outside linebackers Otis Wilson and Wilber Marshall, tattooed passers from September to January.

Chicago breezed to a 12-0 record before falling to Miami in a Monday-night game. That was a mere speed bump for the Bears, who shut out the Giants (21-0) and Rams (24-0) in the playoffs, becoming the first NFL team to post consecutive postseason shutouts in one year.

In Super Bowl XX, the Bears faced the New England Patriots. The underdogs took an early 3-0 lead, but it was all Chicago after that. Ryan's defense dominated, finishing with 7 sacks and 6 takeaways. The Patriots managed just 7 rushing yards on 11 carries.

The final score was Chicago 46, New England 10, and the Bears' prerecorded musical effort, the "Super Bowl Shuffle," echoed throughout the Louisiana Superdome.

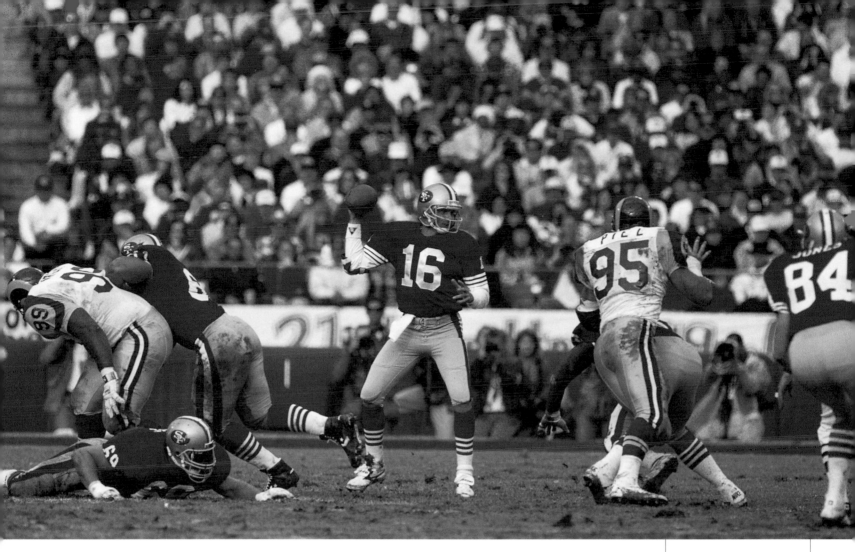

1989
SAN FRANCISCO
49ERS

When the 49ers won their third Super Bowl after the 1988 season, it seemed to mark the end of an era. Bill Walsh, the professorial head coach who skillfully formulated the team's offensive blueprints throughout the 1980s, stepped down after the Super Bowl XXIII victory over Cincinnati.

George Seifert, the defensive coordinator, was promoted to the top spot in 1989, and his team came out of the gate sluggishly. Among San Francisco's first five games, three were narrow victories (over Indianapolis, Tampa Bay, and New Orleans) and another was a 13-12 loss to the Rams.

But the 49ers gained steamed as the season wore on, and the driving force wasn't hard to identify. It was Joe Montana (above), who set an NFL record with a passer rating of 112.4. Montana's completion percentage was an other-

worldly 70.2, and his touchdown-to-interception ratio was 26-8.

Of course, Montana had been a superstar in 1984, too. The biggest difference between that 49ers team and this one was Jerry Rice, who by 1989 had developed into the league's best receiver (82 catches for 1,483 yards and 17 touchdowns). With Roger Craig, a versatile running back, contributing 1,054 yards rushing and 473 receiving (on 49 catches), San Francisco fielded a scorching offense and won 11 of its last 12 games to finish 14-2.

The 49ers made quick work of the NFC playoffs, outscoring the Vikings and Rams by a combined score of 71-16. Montana was not sacked in either game.

Super Bowl XXIV was more of the same. The game was 4 minutes 54 seconds old when Montana hit Rice with a 20-yard touchdown pass. San Francisco scored on six of its first nine possessions against Denver en route to the biggest blowout (55-10) in Super Bowl history. Montana won his third Super Bowl MVP award.

Seifert, rather than tripping in Walsh's shoes, instead became only the second man to win a Super Bowl in his first season as a head coach, joining Don McCafferty (Baltimore, 1970).

Joe Montana (16) enjoyed a dream season in 1989.

AND DEFENSE, TOO
The 1989 San Francisco 49ers are identified with quarterback Joe Montana and a combustible offense that led the league in scoring. But the 49ers' defense deserved some credit, too. The 49ers limited 11 of their 19 opponents to 14 or fewer points, including all three postseason opponents.

1992
DALLAS COWBOYS

HUMBLE BEGINNING
Quarterback Troy Aikman (above), the most valuable player in Super Bowl XXVII, was 0-11 as a starter for the Cowboys in 1989, his rookie season.

When Jerry Jones purchased the Dallas Cowboys in 1989, one of his first acts was to fire head coach Tom Landry—perhaps the most popular figure in Texas since Sam Houston—and replace him with Jimmy Johnson, Jones's old college teammate at Arkansas. When Dallas went 1-15 in its first season in the new regime, the citizens of Dallas went looking for tar and feathers.

But Johnson had a plan, as well as an eye for talent. The Cowboys took quarterback Troy Aikman with the first pick in the 1989 draft. In 1990, they drafted running back Emmitt Smith and traded away one of their few stars, Herschel Walker, getting several key players and draft picks in return. They added tight end Jay Novacek as a free agent, and, in 1992, brought in defensive end Charles Haley via a trade with the 49ers.

The improvement was rapid. The Cowboys went 7-9 in 1990 and 11-5 in 1991. By 1992, the Cowboys were a power to be reckoned with.

Aikman had a productive year, making good use of wide receiver Michael Irvin (one of the few holdovers from the Landry era). But the offense clearly rode on the shoulders of Smith, a short and stocky, between-the-tackles runner who rushed for 1,713 yards and scored 18 touchdowns. Defensively, the Cowboys' calling card was team speed, with Haley and linebacker Ken Norton leading the pack.

After storming through the regular season with a 13-3 record, Dallas polished off Philadelphia 34-10 in a divisional playoff game. But taking the NFC crown meant traveling to San Francisco, where the 49ers (14-2) lay in wait. The Cowboys broke away for a 30-20 victory that sent them to Super Bowl XXVII.

There they thoroughly frustrated the 11-5 Buffalo Bills, forcing an unthinkable 9 turnovers—5 fumbles, 4 interceptions—en route to a 52-17 victory. Dallas would win two more titles in the next three years, marking the rebirth of "America's Team."

1994
SAN FRANCISCO
49ERS

No matter how many games they won together, George Seifert and Steve Young could not climb out of the shadows.

Seifert coached the San Francisco 49ers to victory in Super Bowl XXIV, but most observers thought of it as Bill Walsh's team, in terms of both personnel and philosophy. The situation was similar for Young, who, despite several outstanding seasons at quarterback, constantly was reminded that he wasn't Joe Montana.

They, and the rest of the 49ers, chased away the shadows in 1994. After watching the Dallas Cowboys win back-to-back titles in 1992-93, San Francisco set out to upgrade its roster, adding linebacker-defensive end Rickey Jackson, linebacker Ken Norton, center Bart Oates, and inimitable cornerback Deion Sanders.

The 1994 team scored a club-record 505 points, but it took a while to get rolling. After a humiliating 40-8 home loss to the Eagles, the 49ers stood at 3-2. Rather than a trap door, that defeat proved to be a turning point. San Francisco won its next 10 games and finished 13-3.

Young led the NFL in passing for the fourth year in a row (an unprecedented feat), compiling a record-setting rating of 112.8. The defense ranked second in the league against the rush, and Sanders made his presence felt by returning 3 interceptions for scores.

In the divisional playoffs, the 49ers blasted the Bears 44-15 behind running back Ricky Watters, who scored 5 touchdowns, an NFL postseason record. The 49ers and Cowboys met in the NFC Championship Game for the third successive year, but this time San Francisco left nothing to chance. The 49ers jumped to a 21-0 first-quarter lead and held on for a 38-28 victory.

Two weeks later, Seifert's team made quick work of the San Diego Chargers in Super Bowl XXIX. On the third play of the game, Young hit Jerry Rice with a 44-yard touchdown pass—the first of 6 scoring passes by the left-hander. The 49ers breezed to a 49-26 victory, becoming the first team to win five Super Bowls.

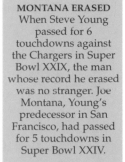

MONTANA ERASED
When Steve Young passed for 6 touchdowns against the Chargers in Super Bowl XXIX, the man whose record he erased was no stranger. Joe Montana, Young's predecessor in San Francisco, had passed for 5 touchdowns in Super Bowl XXIV.

The 49ers ended the Cowboys' reign in the 1994 NFC title game.

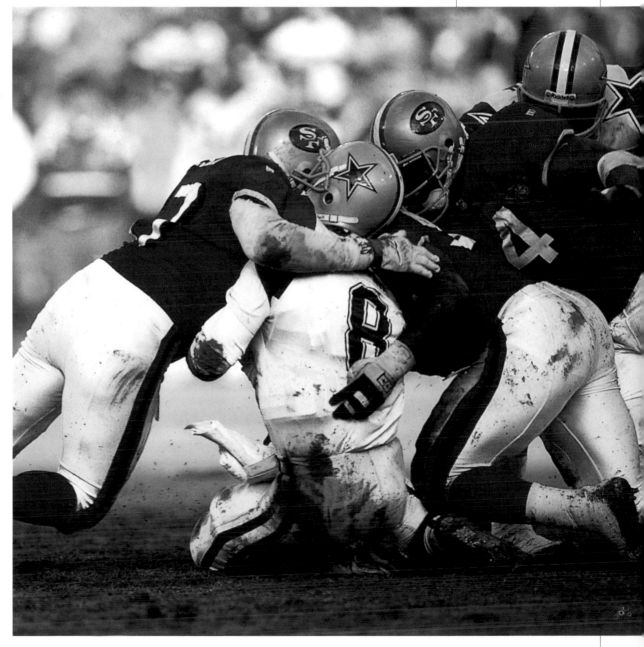

1996
GREEN BAY PACKERS

The Green Bay Packers had only five winning seasons from 1968-1991, making the dynasty of Vince Lombardi seem like a distant memory.

The situation began to change in 1992, the club's first full year under general manager Ron Wolf. One of his first moves was to hire Mike Holmgren, the 49ers' offensive coordinator, as head coach. One of their first moves together was to trade with Atlanta for quarterback Favre. The next year, Green Bay signed all-pro defensive end Reggie White as a free agent.

By 1996, the Packers had become the NFL's best team. Favre, the wild-eyed leader, earned league MVP honors for the second consecutive season by completing nearly 60 percent of his passes for 3,899 yards and 39 touchdowns. He lost his favorite receiver, Robert Brooks, to a knee injury, and temporarily was without his number-two man, Antonio Freeman. But with Favre distributing the passes, it barely mattered.

The Packers weren't one-dimensional, though. They averaged 150 rushing yards in their last six games (including postseason). The defense allowed the fewest yards and points in the NFL. (Green Bay became the first team since the 1972 Dolphins to lead the league both in points scored and fewest allowed.) One more plus: Desmond Howard returned kicks.

Howard returned 3 punts for touchdowns during the regular season, and in a playoff game with San Francisco, he scored or set up the first 2 touchdowns in a 35-14 victory.

After a 30-13 victory against upstart Carolina in the NFC title game, the Packers met the Patriots in Super Bowl XXXI. Howard, who equaled a Super Bowl record with 244 total return yards, delivered the knockout blow on a 99-yard kickoff return for a touchdown in the third quarter. Favre passed for 246 yards, and Green Bay won 35-21.

In 1996, the cannon arm and go-for-broke style of Brett Favre (4) propelled Green Bay to its first NFL title in nearly three decades.

1998
DENVER BRONCOS

When Denver beat Green Bay in Super Bowl XXXII, it ended 13 years of NFC dominance and the Broncos' string of four Super Bowl losses. It was a grand moment for a squad that entered the 1997 postseason as a wild-card team and pulled off several upsets.

The 1998 team, by contrast, didn't surprise anybody. It thrived under the pressure of defending its Super Bowl title and smoked the competition from dawn till midnight.

Curiously, the 1998 offseason was filled with dread for Denver's fans. John Elway, the revered quarterback who had punctuated his career with the victory in Super Bowl XXXII, contemplated retirement for months before finally deciding to play another year.

With Elway back in the starter's role—Bubby Brister replaced him for four games

when injuries struck—coach Mike Shanahan's Broncos set club records for points (501) and total yards (6,092). The 38-year-old Elway had his best season, passing for 22 touchdowns and throwing only 10 interceptions. He was aided considerably by the performance of running back Terrell Davis, who became only the fourth NFL player to rush for more than 2,000 yards in a season (2,008, with 21 touchdowns).

Denver won its first 13 games before falling to the Giants in a last-minute thriller. When the Broncos lost at Miami the next week, questions arose about the team going flat.

The Broncos abolished such thoughts in the playoffs, dispatching the Dolphins, Jets, and Falcons to wrap up their second straight title. Davis rushed for 199, 167, and 102 yards, respectively, setting an NFL postseason record with seven consecutive 100-yard games. Elway passed for 336 yards in the 34-19 victory over Atlanta in Super Bowl XXXIII, earning MVP honors in his final game.

Elway rode into the sunset after directing the best team of his 16-year career with the Broncos.

Denver won a second successive title thanks in large part to Terrell Davis (30), whose 1998 performance ranks among the greatest ever.

FIVE-TIMER
Playing in a Super Bowl often is described as the highlight of a player's career. For John Elway, it was old hat. When he appeared in Super Bowl XXXIII, it was his fifth start in the big game, the most of any quarterback. His Broncos were losers in games XXI, XXII, and XXIV, and winners in games XXXII and XXXIII. He averaged nearly a Super Bowl every three years in his 16-year career.

25
GREATEST
GAMES
OF ALL TIME

NEVERS 40, BEARS 6
November 28, 1929

Ernie Nevers pitched for the St. Louis Browns, played 29 pro football games in one autumn, dabbled in pro basketball, retired to become a coach, and returned to the NFL—all by age 26. That was only a warm-up for what he would accomplish on November 28, 1929.

On that day, the Chicago Cardinals met the Bears in their annual Thanksgiving Day game. Nevers, who returned to the NFL in 1929 after a one-year retirement, made the Cardinals respectable. He also gave them a star to match the Bears' Red Grange. Newspapers in Chicago billed the game as a showdown between Grange and Nevers.

Instead, it turned out to be Nevers's show, as George Halas wrote in his autobiography, *Bears 6, Nevers 40!* The Cardinals' star, plowing straight ahead because of the slick field, scored all 40 of his team's points on 6 touchdowns (all runs less than 20 yards) and 4 extra-point kicks.

Nevers's single-game record for most touchdowns has been equaled, but his mark of 40 points has not been matched. It is the NFL's oldest record.

THE SACKING OF WASHINGTON
December 8, 1940

For Washington, the only disaster comparable to the 1940 NFL Championship Game occurred more than a century earlier, when the British burned the city during the War of 1812.

Unlike the British, who provided ample warning, the Bears offered no indication of the havoc they would wreak—a 73-0 humiliation of the Redskins. Washington had beaten Chicago 7-3 during the regular season, though not

HERO AT REST
Ernie Nevers took a seat for this photo, but "The Blond Blizzard" rarely rested during the 1920s.

Running back Bill Osmanski (9) and the Bears scored virtually at will against the Redskins in a 73-0 championship-game victory.

without recriminations. The Bears argued that a Redskins' defender had interfered with their receiver in the end zone on the game's final play. Redskins owner George Preston Marshall replied that the Bears were "crybabies" and quitters, and boasted that the Redskins' defense had deciphered the Bears' vaunted T-formation.

The Bears seethed while waiting for another shot at the Redskins, which came three weeks later at Washington on December 8. Bears coach George Halas, with some help from special assistant Clark Shaughnessy, crafted a game plan to exploit the Redskins' defense. He correctly anticipated that the Redskins would make few changes to their defensive alignment.

Halas's adjustments produced 3 touchdowns in the first 13 minutes, including Bill Osmanski's 68-yard run on the game's second play. Chicago led 28-0 at halftime, then the Bears' defense returned 3 interceptions for touchdowns to help build a 54-0 third-quarter lead.

Three more touchdowns followed in the fourth quarter. The onslaught became so bad that the officials asked the Bears to stop kicking extra points—the footballs were not being returned from the stands and there was only one left. The Bears obliged by calling passes for their last two conversion attempts.

The New York Times summed it up best: "The weather was perfect. So were the Bears."

defending NFL champion Philadelphia Eagles and the Cleveland Browns, who won the only four AAFC titles. A Super Bowl-like atmosphere surrounded the game, prompting the Eagles to move it from Shibe Park to the larger Municipal Stadium, and prompting the NFL to move it from Sunday afternoon to Saturday night.

NFL owners assumed that older league's dominance would be on display. Instead, a packed house of 71,237 spectators witnessed the unexpected extension of the Browns' dynasty.

Fullback Marion Motley (above) and the Cleveland Browns ran roughshod over the defending NFL champions.

A PREHISTORIC 'SUPER BOWL'
September 16, 1950

During the brief existence of the All-America Football Conference (1946-49), its backers clamored for a game between the AAFC champion and the NFL champion. They finally got their wish—after the AAFC folded and three of its teams joined the NFL.

Thanks to NFL Commissioner Bert Bell, the 1950 season opener matched the two-time

Cleveland coach Paul Brown saw to that. To beat Philadelphia's famed "Eagle" defense, Brown spread the field and went to the air. Browns quarterback Otto Graham fired scoring strikes of 59 yards (to Dub Jones), 26 yards (to Dante Lavelli), and 12 yards (to Mac Speedie) to give Cleveland a 21-3 third-quarter lead.

After the Eagles closed to 21-10, the Browns turned to their running game and ground out 2 more touchdowns for a 35-10 victory. Cleveland dominated in every phase, led by Graham, who passed for 346 yards. After the game, Bell told Brown that the coach had the best team Bell ever had seen. The rest of the NFL soon would subscribe to that view, too.

A TITLE GAME FOR THE AGES

December 24, 1950

After a 10-2 season and a playoff victory over the Giants, the Cleveland Browns were poised to claim the NFL title in 1950, their first year in the league. Only the visiting Los Angeles Rams, who had relocated from Cleveland five years earlier, stood in their way. The fireworks that followed on December 24 produced one of the most memorable NFL Championship Games.

The Rams, who averaged 38.8 points per game during the regular season (still the highest mark ever), struck quickly. On the first play from scrimmage, Bob Waterfield (who led the Cleveland Rams to the 1945 NFL title) teamed with halfback Glenn Davis on an 82-yard touchdown pass play. The Rams also scored on a 3-yard run by Dick Hoerner, but Cleveland countered with 2 touchdown passes by Otto Graham during a back-and-forth first half. Nevertheless, Cleveland trailed 14-13 at halftime because of a botched snap on an extra-point attempt.

In the third quarter, Graham's 39-yard scoring pass to Dante Lavelli gave Cleveland a 20-14 lead. The Rams turned to the 6-foot 4-inch, 220-pound Hoerner, who carried seven consecutive times on the next drive. His second touchdown run gave the visitors a 21-20 lead late in the third quarter. Twenty-one seconds later, the Rams upped their advantage to 28-20 when Larry Brink picked up Marion Motley's fumble and ran 6 yards for a touchdown.

Early in the fourth quarter, momentum swung back to Cleveland when Warren Lahr intercepted Waterfield's pass at the Browns' 35. Graham, who passed for 298 yards, worked the middle of the field for 5 consecutive passes to Lavelli and converted 2 fourth-down plays. Graham finished the drive with his fourth touchdown pass on a 14-yard toss to Rex Bumgardner, who made a diving catch in the end zone with 4:35 left. Suddenly, the Browns had cut their deficit to 28-27.

Cleveland's last chance came with 1:50 remaining. Starting from the Browns' 32-yard line, Graham executed the two-minute drill to perfection. He ran for 14 yards and completed passes of 15, 16, and 12 yards to position Lou Groza for the winning 16-yard field goal with 28 seconds left. Lahr's second interception moments later sealed Cleveland's 30-28 victory.

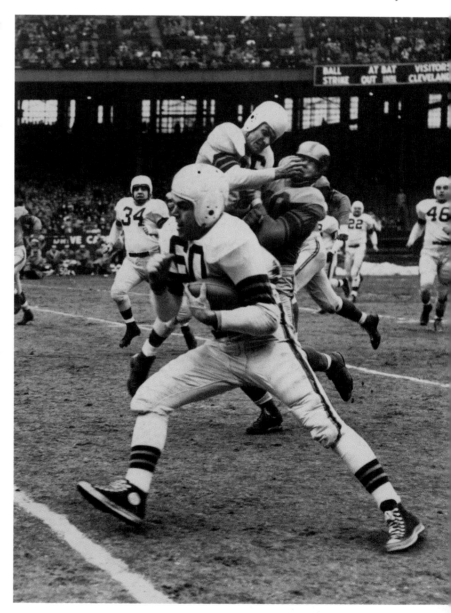

Otto Graham (60), clad in sneakers because of the frozen field, directed the Browns to a thrilling victory in the 1950 title game.

RUNAWAY TRUCK
While Otto Graham directed a high-powered passing attack for the 1950 Cleveland Browns, bulldozing fullback Marion Motley (above) supplied the ground game. Motley led the league in rushing in 1950 with 810 yards—while averaging 5.8 yards per carry.

DYNAMIC DUO
Otto Graham and Dante Lavelli (above) teamed on 366 completions during their 10 seasons together, plus countless other collaborations during the playoffs. In the 1950 NFL title game, Lavelli caught a record 11 passes from Graham for 128 yards and 2 touchdowns.

A Legend Is Born

December 28, 1958

Many consider Johnny Unitas the greatest quarterback ever. For all of the records he posted during his 18-year career (1956-1973), he always will be remembered best for his fantastic finishes. The birth of that legend can be traced to one day: the 1958 NFL Championship Game, known as the "Greatest Game Ever Played."

Twelve future Hall of Fame members played that afternoon at Yankee Stadium, and none shone brighter than Unitas. His passing and play calling propelled the Colts to a 14-3 halftime lead, and, midway through the third quarter, they seemed en route to a blowout when they marched to the Giants' 1-yard line.

On fourth down, however, the Giants stopped running back Alan Ameche, and quarterback Charlie Conerly then led New York on a 95-yard touchdown drive that included an 86-yard gain on a fumbled pass completion. Four minutes later, Conerly hit Frank Gifford for a 15-yard touchdown pass early in the fourth quarter to give the Giants a 17-14 lead.

The Giants still were nursing that advantage when Gifford got the call on third-and-4 from New York's 40-yard line. Gino Marchetti, Baltimore's stellar defensive end, suffered a broken leg on the play, but not before he made the tackle. The officials spotted the ball just short of the first down, though to this day Gifford swears he made the necessary yards.

After a punt, the Colts took possession at their 14-yard line with 1:56 remaining. The Giants figured Unitas had to go to the sidelines or go deep. Unitas exploited the middle of the field. On third-and-10, he found Lenny Moore for 11 yards. After an incompletion, he teamed with Raymond Berry on 3 consecutive passes, covering 62 yards, to set up Steve Myhra's game-tying field goal with seven seconds left.

The unflappable Unitas starred again in overtime, marching the Colts 80 yards to the game-winning touchdown. He kept the Giants off balance by mixing runs and passes. On third-and-14, Unitas found Berry for a 21-yard gain to the Giants' 42, then handed off on a draw to Ameche, who ran for 22 yards. Ameche finished the job with a dramatic 1-yard plunge for the winning touchdown.

When Alan Ameche (above) plunged into the end zone, the Colts were NFL champions.

SUDDEN DEATH
When a modern NFL game is tied at the end of regulation time, no one is surprised to see the contest resumed with a sudden-death overtime period. But the concept was new in 1958. The ball commemorating that NFL "first" is on display in the Pro Football Hall of Fame.

EAGLES SOAR ON DUTCHMAN'S ARM

December 26, 1960

The 1960 NFL Championship Game, played at Philadelphia's Franklin Field, matched teams headed in different directions. While Green Bay would reign for the rest of the decade, and Philadelphia would not reach the postseason again for 18 years, this day belonged to the Eagles.

The young Packers were loaded, while the veteran Eagles were so depleted their all-pro center (35-year-old Chuck Bednarik) had to play linebacker, too. Philadelphia had an anemic running attack, and only one team allowed more rushing yards. Yet the Eagles went 10-2, thanks largely to the leadership and play of Bednarik and 34-year-old quarterback Norm Van Brocklin, who was appearing in his final game. "[Van Brocklin] taught the Eagles to be winners," said flanker Tommy McDonald.

The day followed the Eagles' script: Their defense bent but did not break, and the offense produced big plays. Trailing 6-0 in the second quarter, Van Brocklin teamed with McDonald on consecutive passes of 22 and 35 yards, the latter resulting in a touchdown and a 7-6 lead. A field goal gave the Eagles a 10-6 halftime lead.

Though the Packers continued to move the ball at will (they ran 29 more plays than the Eagles, outgaining them 401-296), Philadelphia's lead held up until the fourth quarter when Bart Starr found Max McGee for a 7-yard touchdown pass. Ted Dean took the ensuing kickoff and returned it 58 yards to the Packers' 39. A 13-yard pass by Van Brocklin set up Dean's 5-yard touchdown run with 9:39 left, which gave Philadelphia a 17-13 lead.

The Packers' next drive ended with a fumble (caused by Bednarik). In the final seconds, Green Bay drove to the Eagles' 22. Starr completed a pass to Jim Taylor over the middle, but Bednarik, the one man between Taylor and the end zone, wrapped him up at the 8-yard line, and kept him on the ground as time expired.

"You can get up now," Bednarik said to Taylor. "You just lost."

SAYERS IS UNSTOPPABLE

December 12, 1965

On a miserable day for football, rain turned Wrigley Field into slop, and the San Francisco 49ers and Chicago Bears girded for what promised to be a tough day of slogging through the mud.

Not for Gale Sayers, however. The "Kansas Comet" seemingly glided over the mess to deliver one of the greatest performances in NFL history.

It began with a screen pass in the first quarter, when a marvelous move sprang Sayers for an 80-yard touchdown. Four more trips to the end zone followed—on runs of 21, 7, 50, and 1 yards—until Bears coach George Halas sat down his rookie halfback after three quarters.

Gale Sayers (40) leaves two 49ers in his wake en route to an 80-yard touchdown reception.

That left Sayers 1 touchdown short of the NFL record, shared by the Cardinals' Ernie Nevers and the Browns' Dub Jones, and the Bears' fans let Halas know it. The coach would not budge, even when Chicago had the ball at the 49ers' 1-yard line.

Anyway, that would have been too easy for Sayers, who went for the spectacular instead. After Halas sent him back out to return a punt, Sayers fielded the ball at his 15-yard line and ran right. He shed one tackler, then cut back at midfield and raced down the left sideline for his record-tying sixth touchdown.

That play capped a brilliant exhibition by Sayers, who had 336 all-purpose yards—113 on 9 carries, 89 on 2 receptions, and 134 on 4 punt returns—in a 61-20 victory. "It seemed like everyone was slipping but me," Sayers said.

A PACKERS-COWBOYS CLASSIC
January 1, 1967

When the Dallas Cowboys advanced to the 1966 NFL Championship Game, they were not expected to put up much of a fight against the Green Bay Packers. After all, the Packers were considered one of the greatest teams ever, having already won three NFL titles during the 1960s. Meanwhile, the Cowboys, just six years removed from expansion status, were making their first postseason appearance.

The Packers made it look easy in the early going at the Cotton Bowl. Bart Starr's 17-yard touchdown pass to Elijah Pitts and Jim Grabowski's 18-yard fumble return gave Green Bay a 14-0 first-quarter lead. Dallas did not fold, however, and in a pattern that would be repeated all day, roared back to tie the score before quarter's end.

The Packers regained the lead on Starr's 51-yard bomb to Carroll Dale. Back came the Cowboys, with field goals in the second and third quarters that cut the Packers' lead to 21-20. Starr (19 of 28 for 304 yards and 4 touchdowns) answered, firing a 16-yard scoring pass to Boyd Dowler and a 28-yard touchdown to Max McGee. The latter score came with 5:20 left, but the Cowboys blocked the extra-point attempt to stay alive at 34-20.

Back came the Cowboys again. A minute later, Don Meredith found Frank Clarke for a 68-yard touchdown pass that made the score 34-27. Dallas's defense limited the Packers to three downs and out, and, after a 16-yard punt, the Cowboys took over on Green Bay's 47 with 2:19 left. Meredith's passing and a 20-yard pass interference penalty gave Dallas the ball at Green Bay's 2-yard line with 1:52 remaining. One play later the Cowboys were at the 1, and a tying touchdown appeared imminent.

That touchdown never came. A false start on second down moved Dallas back to the 6. A pass by Meredith got the Cowboys to the 2-yard line, but on fourth down, Green Bay safety Tom Brown intercepted Meredith's pass in the end zone to preserve Green Bay's 34-27 victory.

CLUTCH PLAYER
Max McGee caught only 4 passes during the 1966 season, but he proved instrumental to the Packers' postseason run. His touchdown against Dallas turned out to be the game winner, and, two weeks later in Super Bowl I, he came off the bench to catch 7 passes for 138 yards and 2 touchdowns.

GOAT TO HERO
The Cowboys reached the Packers' 1-yard line late in the 1966 title game thanks largely to a pass interference penalty against Green Bay's Dave Robinson. But the linebacker redeemed himself moments later when he pressured Don Meredith, forcing the Cowboys' quarterback into an interception.

THE ICE BOWL
December 31, 1967

How cold was it in Green Bay on the final day of 1967? So cold that it froze the heating grid under Lambeau Field, which was designed to keep the field from freezing.

But not cold enough to stop the 1967 NFL Championship Game, despite the secret hopes of many players. So, even as the temperature read 13-below zero and the wind-chill factor reached 48 degrees below zero, the Dallas Cowboys took the field against the Packers.

Once the NFL decided the show must go on, so did the Packers. Quarterback Bart Starr teamed with end Boyd Dowler on touchdown passes of 8 and 46 yards to stake Green Bay to a 14-0 second-quarter lead.

But Dallas defensive end George Andrie scooped up Starr's fumble and ran 7 yards for a touchdown, and the Cowboys also added a field goal to cut the Packers' advantage to 14-10 at halftime. Then, Dallas took its first lead on the opening play of the fourth quarter, when Dan Reeves completed a 50-yard touchdown pass to Lance Rentzel on a halfback option play.

Dallas still led 17-14 when Green Bay took over at its 32 with 4:50 remaining. This was the Packers' last chance, not only for this day but for the dynasty, and the veteran squad mustered one more bit of magic. Starr led the way, mixing runs and passes (he completed 5 of 5 attempts for 59 yards) to move the Packers to the Cowboys' 1-yard line with 30 seconds remaining.

Two plunges into the middle netted no gain, and with 16 seconds left, Starr called the Packers' last time out. The next play seemed likely to be a pass because an incompletion would stop the clock, whereas a failed running play would not allow enough time for Green Bay to attempt a tying field goal.

Starr and coach Vince Lombardi, though, had other ideas. Starr told Lombardi he thought he could sneak it over, and the coach told him: "Then do it, and let's get the hell out of here." On an all-or-nothing play, Starr followed Jerry Kramer's block into the end zone to lift Green Bay to a 21-17 victory. It gave the Packers their fifth NFL title in seven years, and several weeks later, after Green Bay's victory in Super Bowl II, Lombardi retired.

Bart Starr (15) put an end to the Ice Bowl when he dived into the end zone behind the block of Jerry Kramer (64).

Charlie Smith (23) delivered his biggest play after the cameras were turned off.

THE 'HEIDI GAME'
November 17, 1968

What does a sweet little Swiss girl in *dirndl* have to do with pro football? Quite a bit, as it turned out.

A seemingly innocuous decision by an NBC executive—to pre-empt the broadcast of the end of an AFL game for the start of the movie *Heidi*—triggered a fire storm. Better than any poll, it delivered an unmistakable message about the popularity of pro football and America's passionate attachment to the game.

The particulars involved an AFL game between bitter rivals—the New York Jets and

Oakland Raiders—at the Oakland Coliseum on November 17, 1968. The game would serve as a lead-in for *Heidi*, the network's new movie based on the children's book. The game started at 4 P.M. (EST), the movie at 7 P.M.

The Jets and Raiders squared off in a classic AFL shootout tinged by hard feelings. Fights, flags, and big hits dominated a first half that ended with Oakland leading 14-12. In the third quarter, Jets safety Jim Hudson became so enraged that he was ejected. The teams traded scores until New York took a 32-29 lead on Jim Turner's 26-yard field goal with 1:05 remaining in the game.

The timing could not have been better for NBC. The game went to a commercial, and when the break ended, *Heidi* started.

Network executives had cut away, believing New York's lead was safe with so little time remaining. They were wrong. A 20-yard pass by Daryle Lamonica and a 15-yard penalty put the Raiders into Jets territory. Then, halfback Charlie Smith, isolated on Hudson's replacement, ran by the safety and hauled in a 43-yard touchdown pass with 42 seconds left to put Oakland ahead 36-32.

The Raiders were not done, either. On the ensuing kickoff, the Jets' Earl Christy bobbled the ball, and the Raiders swarmed him at the Jets' 10. The ball squirted to the 2, where the Raiders' Preston Ridlehuber recovered and ran in for a touchdown to conclude a 43-32 victory.

The Jets were alternatively shocked and furious, but that was nothing compared to the emotions expressed to the NBC switchboard. So many angry viewers phoned to complain about missing the fantastic ending of a fantastic game that the network issued a public apology.

> *Men who wouldn't get out of their chairs during an earthquake rushed to the phones to scream obscenities.*
>
> Columnist
> Art Buchwald

TROUBLEMAKER
Jennifer Edwards, who played the part of Heidi, got more publicity than she hoped for when the movie in which she appeared pre-empted the end of a classic game between the Oakland Raiders and the New York Jets.

After the Chiefs squandered a chance to win in regulation, Bob Griese (12) and the Dolphins won the NFL's longest game.

> **When I saw [the referee] signal that Garo's field goal was good, I broke out laughing. I was so tired, I just laughed.**
>
> *Bob Griese*

THE LONGEST DAY
December 25, 1971

The Miami Dolphins, just five years removed from expansion status, came to Kansas City's Municipal Stadium for a 1971 AFC Divisional Playoff Game, and, like a terrier, they stuck to the Chiefs' heels all day. In the final two minutes of a 24-24 game, however, Kansas City's Ed Podolak returned a kickoff 78 yards to set up a 32-yard field-goal attempt. With Chiefs standout Jan Stenerud attempting the kick, the 50,374 spectators thought they would be home in time for Christmas dinner.

Stenerud missed wide right by inches, the beginning of a long day's journey into night. After 22 minutes 40 seconds of overtime (and 82 minutes 40 seconds overall), the NFL's longest game finally ended on a 37-yard field goal by the Dolphins' Garo Yepremian.

The game did not begin that way. The Chiefs squandered several opportunities, which allowed the Dolphins to catch them at 10-10, 17-17, and 24-24. Both teams had a chance to win in the first overtime, but Nick Buoniconti blocked Stenerud's 42-yard field-goal attempt and Yepremian missed from 52 yards.

The Dolphins finally broke through in the second overtime period by eschewing their outside running attack, which the Chiefs had stopped cold, and turning to misdirection plays. Fullback Larry Csonka burst up the middle for 29 yards to the Chiefs' 36, and three plays later, Yepremian delivered his winning field goal for a 27-24 victory.

The Chiefs wasted an outstanding day by Podolak, who totaled 350 all-purpose yards (110 receiving, 85 rushing, 155 returning kickoffs). The defeat marked the end of Kansas City's stay among pro football's elite; the Chiefs would not reach the playoffs again for 15 years.

STAUBACH STRIKES
December 23, 1972

In 1970 and 1971, Dallas handed San Francisco a pair of tough postseason defeats. In 1972, the Cowboys delivered the cruelest cut of all.

In an NFC Divisional Playoff Game at San Francisco's Candlestick Park, the 49ers started fast. Vic Washington returned the opening kickoff 97 yards for a touchdown, and 2

touchdown runs by Larry Schreiber gave the 49ers a 21-3 lead.

After Dallas closed to 21-13, Schreiber scored again to make it 28-13. Enter Roger Staubach. The Cowboys' quarterback and Super Bowl VI MVP missed most of the 1972 season with a separated shoulder, but he came off the bench late in the third quarter to jump-start Dallas's offense, producing the first of his legendary fourth-quarter comebacks.

After Staubach led Dallas on a drive to a field goal, the Cowboys trailed 28-16. The score did not change until less than two minutes remained, when Staubach finished a 55-yard drive with a 20-yard touchdown pass to Billy Parks. After Mel Renfro recovered an onside kick, Staubach ran 21 yards, passed to Parks for 19 more, then found Ron Sellers for the winning 10-yard touchdown pass with 52 seconds left. The Cowboys had done it again, winning 30-28.

'IMMACULATE RECEPTION'
December 23, 1972

In 1972, the Pittsburgh Steelers completed their fortieth season by advancing to the playoffs for only the second time. Their first postseason appearance had been brief (a 21-0 loss to Philadelphia in 1947), and these Steelers seemed headed for a similar fate.

With 22 seconds left in an AFC Divisional Playoff Game at Three Rivers Stadium, Pittsburgh trailed Oakland 7-6 and faced fourth-and-10 from its 40-yard line. Art Rooney, the club's owner and founder, headed down the elevator to the locker room to console his team, thereby missing one of the wackiest plays and one of the most fantastic finishes in NFL history.

Pittsburgh quarterback Terry Bradshaw dropped back to pass, but the Raiders flushed him out of the pocket to the right. He saw running back John (Frenchy) Fuqua over the middle at the Raiders' 35, and with defenders closing, Bradshaw fired a pass toward Fuqua.

Fuqua, Raiders safety Jack Tatum, and the ball converged simultaneously, and out popped the ball. The Raiders began to celebrate, not realizing that rookie running back Franco Harris, trailing the play at the Raiders' 42, had picked the ball out of the air at his shoe tops and taken off down the left sideline. Some Raiders gave chase, but they could not stop Harris from running to the end zone.

Touchdown? Nobody knew, including the officials. The Raiders argued that Fuqua had batted the ball to Harris (the rules of the time did not permit consecutive touches by offensive players). If Tatum had batted the ball, the play would have been a touchdown.

Referee Fred Swearingen, after consulting with NFL supervisor of officials Art McNally, came back on the field and ruled the play a touchdown. Pittsburgh kicked the extra point to take a 13-7 lead with five seconds left, a score that was finalized moments later.

For a franchise cursed by a four-decade run of bad luck, the "Immaculate Reception" amounted to an unbelievable dose of good fortune—and a welcome turning point.

A stunning reception by Franco Harris transformed defeat into victory for the Pittsburgh Steelers.

UNSOLVED MYSTERY
Only John (Frenchy) Fuqua knows for sure whether he touched the ball that led to the "Immaculate Reception," and more than 25 years later, he's still not telling. "I want to keep it 'Immaculate,'" Fuqua said in 1999.

Clarence Davis (28) outwrestled three Dolphins defenders to secure Oakland's 28-26 playoff victory.

DOLPHINS' DYNASTY COMES TO AN END
December 21, 1974

The Miami Dolphins, seeking their third consecutive Super Bowl title, came to Oakland to play the Raiders in a 1974 AFC Divisional Playoff Game. A loud and raucous Raiders crowd greeted the Dolphins, then immediately went silent after Miami's Nat Moore returned the opening kickoff 89 yards for a touchdown. That, however, would be only the first blow in a 15-round heavyweight battle.

On a day of spectacular plays, the Raiders produced two of the most spectacular. Fred Biletnikoff reached up with his left hand and snared a high pass from Kenny Stabler while dragging both feet inbounds for a remarkable 13-yard touchdown that gave Oakland a 14-10 lead. Later, Cliff Branch made a diving catch at the Dolphins' 28, and when nobody touched him, he bounced to his feet and raced into the end zone to complete a 72-yard touchdown.

After Branch's effort, Oakland led 21-19, but not for long. The Dolphins covered 68 yards in 4 plays, the last 23 yards on a touchdown run by Benny Malone, to take a 26-21 lead with 2:08 left. That was enough time for Stabler, who led Oakland to the Dolphins' 8 with 35 seconds left.

With no time outs left, the Raiders had to pass, and the Dolphins knew it. Stabler could not find a receiver, so he drifted left, followed by Miami's Vern Den Herder. Just as Den Herder was wrapping him up, Stabler "wristed" the ball in the direction of one Raiders receiver (running back Clarence Davis) and three Dolphins. Somehow Davis won the wrestling match for the ball. His touchdown with 26 seconds left gave Oakland a 28-26 victory, ending the Dolphins' reign.

'HAIL MARY'
December 28, 1975

When a team needs a touchdown and time is running out, it often resorts to a play called the "Hail Mary." The notion is that the quarterback will throw the ball as far as he can, and pray that a teammate catches it.

Amazingly, on December 28, 1975, the desperation play worked.

The visiting Dallas Cowboys, trailing Minnesota 14-10 in a 1975 NFC Divisional Playoff Game, needed a miracle. With only 32 seconds left, they still had 50 yards to cover, and the NFL's best pass defense stood between them and the end zone.

This seemed too great a hurdle even for Dallas quarterback Roger Staubach, a master of fourth-quarter comebacks. He had produced a near miracle to get to midfield when he completed a 25-yard pass to Drew Pearson on fourth-and-16.

Staubach dropped back from the 50 and heaved a high, arcing pass. Pearson and Vikings cornerback Nate Wright, running stride for stride down the right side, both slowed to adjust to the underthrown ball. Then Wright fell down. Pearson penned the ball against his hip with his right hand at the 5-yard line and waltzed into the end zone with 24 seconds left, giving Dallas a 17-14 victory and a trip to the NFC Championship Game.

The Cowboys' desperate prayers were answered when Drew Pearson scored on a "Hail Mary" pass.

STEEL CURTAIN FALLS ON DALLAS

January 18, 1976

No other title game in NFL history provided a greater contrast in styles than Super Bowl X between the Pittsburgh Steelers and Dallas Cowboys.

The Steelers were rough and rugged, the Cowboys sleek and modern. Pittsburgh was old school, Dallas was high tech. On offense, the Steelers liked to line up and run right at teams, while their defense attacked man against man. Dallas relied on deception and technique on both sides of the line of scrimmage.

All those elements would play a role in this battle of old versus new, which kicked off January 18, 1976, at Miami's Orange Bowl. In the main event, Pittsburgh's Steel Curtain

defense limited Dallas to 270 total yards while recording 7 sacks and 3 takeaways. Ultimately, however, no element mattered more than Steelers wide receiver Lynn Swann.

In the first quarter, Swann went up along the sideline and snared a pass over Dallas cornerback Mark Washington. In midair, the Steelers' receiver somehow contorted his body to land inbounds. The 32-yard play set up a touchdown that tied the score 7-7.

Swann's second catch did not lead to any points, but it remains one of the greatest receptions in NFL history. He and Washington went up together, with Swann tipping the ball. As they both tumbled to the ground, and with Washington wrapping up the receiver, Swann maintained his concentration and hauled in a spectacular 53-yard reception.

That only set the stage for the decisive blow, which came with Pittsburgh leading 15-10 late in the fourth quarter. The Cowboys blitzed on third-and-4 from the Steelers' 36, leaving Swann in single coverage. He outran Washington on a post pattern and collected a 64-yard bomb from Terry Bradshaw with 3:02 remaining. Swann's touchdown turned out to be the game winner in a 21-17 victory, and his performance (4 catches for 161 yards) earned him MVP honors.

SUPER RIVALRY
Super Bowl X marked more than a special anniversary for the NFL. It marked the first chapter in a heated rivalry between the Cowboys and the Steelers, who would meet again for the NFL title three years later.

Key receptions by Lynn Swann were the difference in Pittsburgh's victory over Dallas.

The Dolphins had no answer for Earl Campbell (34).

CAMPBELL RUNS WILD

November 20, 1978

During its 30-year run, *Monday Night Football* has featured numerous thrillers and great games. The 1978 contest between the Miami Dolphins and Houston Oilers may have been the best of the lot.

Houston, which had not made a Monday night appearance in two years, owed its prime-time invitation to its star rookie running back, Earl Campbell. The "Tyler Rose" had overpowered opponents and brought the Oilers back to respectability. On this night, he would thrust himself and the team into the spotlight.

Campbell rushed for only 44 yards in the first half, but his second touchdown of the game provided the Oilers with a 21-14 lead in the third quarter. After Miami rallied to regain the lead at 23-21, Campbell took center stage. The 235-pound running back was a workhorse on an 80-yard drive to the go-ahead touchdown, which came on his 12-yard run with 4:46 remaining in the game.

Houston forced Miami to punt on the next possession, and the Oilers, leading 28-23, took over at their 19-yard line with 1:22 left. The Dolphins needed to regain possession; instead, they got Campbell on a sweep. Displaying uncommon speed for a man his size, Campbell raced around the Dolphins' defense and sprinted the rest of the way for an 81-yard touchdown. He wound up with 28 carries for 199 yards in Houston's 35-30 victory.

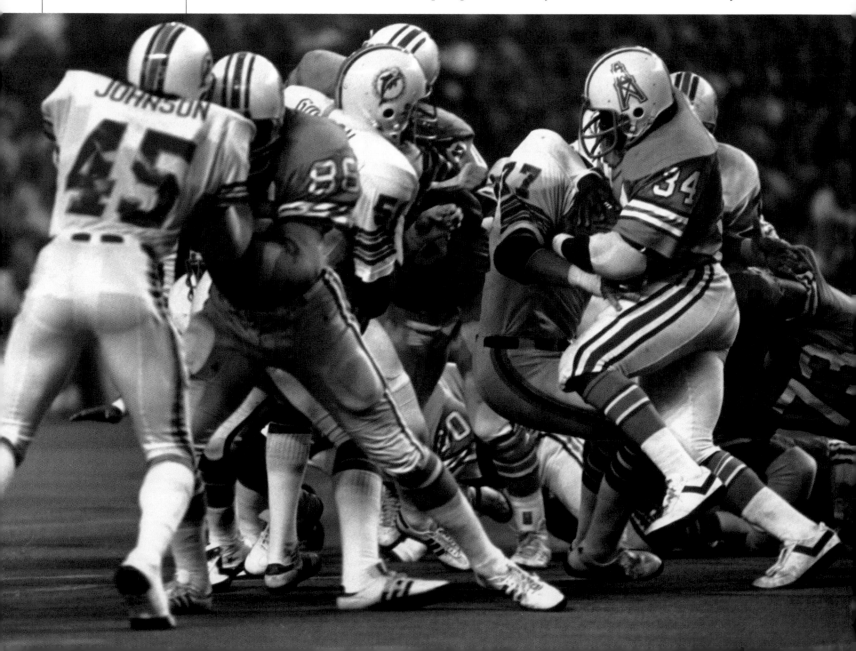

SUPER BOWL XIII

January 21, 1979

Seven months after *Jaws 2* opened, the Super Bowl also produced a sequel, only it played to better reviews. The Steelers and Cowboys, who battled so ferociously in Super Bowl X, returned to Miami's Orange Bowl for a renewal of their bitter rivalry.

The defending-champion Dallas Cowboys brought a better team into Super Bowl XIII. Unfortunately for Dallas, so did Pittsburgh. The Cowboys' roster included several key additions since Super Bowl X, headlined by second-year running back Tony Dorsett. The Steelers' improvement rested not so much on player changes but on the upgraded performance of quarterback Terry Bradshaw.

Bradshaw, who had mostly played a supporting role during the Steelers' first two title runs, moved into the spotlight in 1978. The confident and daring quarterback led Pittsburgh to a 14-2 record and playoff victories over Denver and Houston. With the Steelers' running game bottled up, Bradshaw would play a pivotal role against Dallas.

Bradshaw passed for 253 yards in the first half, including touchdowns of 28 and 75 yards to wide receiver John Stallworth, to stake Pittsburgh to a 21-14 advantage. After Dallas closed to 21-17, Bradshaw led the Steelers on an 85-yard drive that culminated in Franco Harris's 22-yard touchdown run with 7:10 remaining in the game. On Harris's run, Bradshaw, reading blitz, changed the play from a pass to a draw, and Harris ran untouched through the Cowboys' defense.

The Steelers recovered a fumble on the ensuing kickoff, and in typical Bradshaw style, he went for broke, firing an 18-yard touchdown pass to Lynn Swann. Bradshaw threw high and hard over the middle—in other words, a perfect pass because only the soaring Swann could catch it.

That score, coming with 6:51 remaining, increased Pittsburgh's advantage to 35-17. Dallas scored twice in the final minutes, but Rocky Bleier recovered an onside kick with 22 seconds left to secure a 35-31 victory and the Steelers' unprecedented third Super Bowl title.

Bradshaw (17 of 30 for 318 yards and 4 touchdowns) earned the first of two consecutive Super Bowl MVP awards, and Swann (7 catches for 124 yards and 1 touchdown) sparkled again.

Terry Bradshaw was named Super Bowl XIII MVP after passing for 318 yards and 4 touchdowns.

FALLEN HERO
Jackie Smith, who had starred for the Cardinals, came out of retirement to join Dallas in 1978—only to a drop a touchdown pass in Super Bowl XIII.

Exhausted at the end of a fierce battle against the Dolphins, the Chargers' Kellen Winslow was helped from the field by Billy Shields (left) and Eric Sievers.

BIG MAN
Kellen Winslow had the game of a lifetime against the Dolphins, setting an NFL playoff record by catching 13 passes for 166 yards and 1 touchdown. No play mattered more, though, than his game-saving tip of Uwe von Schamann's 43-yard field-goal attempt at the end of regulation.

A FIGHT TO THE FINISH IN MIAMI
January 2, 1982

The 1981 AFC Divisional Playoff Game between the San Diego Chargers and the Miami Dolphins had everything: wacky plays, heroic performances, endless drama, and countless momentum swings in the humid heat of Miami. No wonder many consider it the greatest game in pro football history, the 1958 NFL Championship Game notwithstanding.

With a trip to the AFC title game on the line, the Chargers jumped to a 24-0 first-quarter lead. That forced the Dolphins to abandon their conservative game plan and bring in veteran quarterback Don Strock. Passing on almost every down, Strock led the Dolphins to 10 points while the Chargers' high-powered offense stalled. Still, San Diego had a 24-10 advantage as halftime neared—until Miami produced lightning.

The Dolphins, without much time (six seconds) or much hope of getting another score

before intermission (they were at the Chargers' 40), called a play that usually only works on the sandlot, then executed it perfectly. Strock fired a pass to Duriel Harris on the right side at San Diego's 25. As Chargers defenders hurried to make the tackle and end the half, Harris lateraled the ball to Tony Nathan, who streaked past the Chargers' stunned defense to complete a 40-yard touchdown.

The "Hook and Ladder" play made it 24-17, and sent the Dolphins into the locker room on an emotional high that carried over into the second half. Strock, who passed for 403 yards and 4 touchdowns, led Miami on scoring drives of 74 and 83 yards. In between, Dan Fouts guided the Chargers on a 60-yard march. The teams were tied 31-31 as the third quarter wound down.

But not for long. An interception late in the period gave Miami the ball at San Diego's 15, and on the first play of the fourth quarter, Nathan scored on a 12-yard run. The Dolphins, once on the verge of being blown out, had their first lead.

They almost put the game away with a seven-minute drive, but momentum swung again when San Diego's Willie Shaw recovered a fumble at the Chargers' 18 with 4:39 left. Fouts then completed 7 of 8 passes for 75 yards, including a 9-yard touchdown to James Brooks that tied the game 38-38 with 58 seconds left. Back came Strock, who led Miami to the Chargers' 25 with four seconds left. But Kellen Winslow, San Diego's 6-foot 5-inch tight end, tipped Uwe von Schamann's attempt at a winning 43-yard field goal and the teams went to overtime.

In overtime, after each team missed a potential winning field goal (von Schamann had another kick blocked), Fouts, who completed 33 of 53 passes for 433 yards and 3 touchdowns, found Charlie Joiner for a 39-yard pass. That play capped a 74-yard drive and set up Rolf Benirschke's 29-yard field goal to end the game after 13:52 of overtime.

'THE CATCH'
January 10, 1982

The game known for "The Catch" involved so much more than that. For the NFL, it marked a changing of the guard.

Entering the scene were the 49ers, who went on to win Super Bowl XVI, the first of San Francisco's four NFL titles during the 1980s. Exiting the scene were the Cowboys, one of the league's most dominant teams throughout the 1970s. The transition began with a leaping fingertip grab by Dwight Clark that propelled San Francisco to a 28-27 victory over Dallas in the 1981 NFC Championship Game at San Francisco's Candlestick Park.

The 49ers announced their ascension to the league's elite during the 1981 regular season when they blasted Dallas 45-14. They started fast in the title game, taking the opening kickoff and driving 63 yards to a touchdown on an 8-yard pass from Joe Montana to Freddie Solomon. The Cowboys countered with 10 points, the touchdown coming after they recovered a 49ers' fumble.

Back and forth they went. Montana's 20-yard touchdown pass to Clark gave San Francisco a 14-10 lead, but Dallas answered with an 80-yard touchdown drive to take a 17-14 halftime advantage. In the third quarter, both teams struggled with turnovers, one of which San Francisco turned into a touchdown for a fragile 21-17 lead entering the final period.

Dallas scored 10 points in the first five minutes of the fourth quarter. First, Rafael Septien kicked a field goal, then another 49ers turnover (they had 6 in the game) paved the way for the go-ahead touchdown on Danny White's 21-yard pass to Doug Cosbie. An interception ended the 49ers' next possession, and their dream season appeared to be ending, too.

San Francisco got another chance, though, taking over at its 11 with 4:54 remaining. Montana, utilizing running plays and short passes, led the 49ers to the Cowboys' 6-yard line with 58 seconds left. On third-and-3, the 49ers called Sprint Right Option, a play that produced their first touchdown on the pass to Solomon.

Montana rolled right, but Solomon could not get open. Just as the quarterback was about to be flattened, he lofted a high pass. At first, it appeared that he had thrown the ball away, but Clark, running along the back of the end zone, climbed an imaginary ladder to make an unforgettable reception with 51 seconds left.

"I don't know how he got it," said Montana. "He can't jump that high."

The Cowboys, however, were not finished yet. White completed a 31-yard strike to Drew Pearson, and only a one-handed tackle by cornerback Eric Wright saved a touchdown and the game. The 49ers finally ended the Cowboys' hopes when Lawrence Pillers sacked White, forcing a fumble that defensive end Jim Stuckey recovered at the 50-yard line. The Team of the 1980s was on its way.

This dramatic catch by Dwight Clark in the back of the end zone propelled the 49ers past Dallas and on to the Super Bowl.

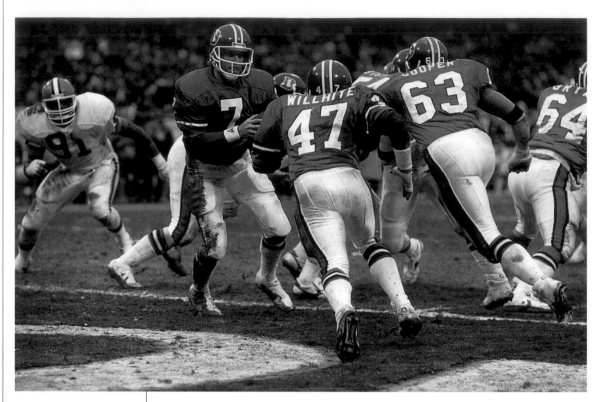

John Elway (7) began "The Drive" in the shadow of the Broncos' end zone.

punted. Starting from his 25, Elway completed passes of 22 and 28 yards to set up Rich Karlis's game-winning 33-yard field goal 5:48 into the extra period. What remains etched in every fan's mind, though, is the 15-play, 98-yard march that has taken its place in NFL lore as the most famous drive in history. The day that the Broncos' all-star quarterback engineered "The Drive" is the day he cemented his status as the master of the comeback.

"When you've got John Elway on your team," Broncos coach Dan Reeves said, "you've always got a chance. Always."

John Elway (7) began "The Drive" in the shadow of the Broncos' end zone.

> **"**
> *When you've got John Elway on your team, you've always got a chance. Always.*
> **"**
>
> Dan Reeves

'THE DRIVE'
January 11, 1987

Trailing the Cleveland Browns 20-13 with 5 minutes 32 seconds remaining in the 1986 AFC Championship Game, the Denver Broncos were a long way from scoring (they had 98 yards between them and the end zone) and seemingly short on hope.

But as they knew, and the rest of the NFL would discover, anything is possible with John Elway at quarterback.

Elway started cautiously, with a pass and three runs, to give Denver breathing room. Then he scrambled for 11 yards and fired a 22-yard pass to running back Steve Sewell and a 12-yard pass to wide receiver Steve Watson. The capacity crowd in Cleveland was starting to get nervous, but a sack left the Broncos facing third-and-18 from the Browns' 48 with 1:47 left.

No problem for Elway, who connected with wide receiver Mark Jackson on a 20-yard strike. Another pass to Sewell and another run by Elway left Denver facing third-and-1 at the Browns' 5 with 39 seconds left. The Browns came on a blitz, and Elway delivered another perfect shot, low and hard to a sliding Jackson for the tying 5-yard touchdown.

In overtime, the Browns took possession first, but then went three downs and out and

SUPER BOWL XXIII
January 22, 1989

Of the 49ers' four Super Bowl championship teams during the 1980s, the 1988 squad may have been the most improbable. The team staggered much of the season, regrouped to

make the playoffs, then stunned the Bears in Chicago to win the NFC title game.

That brought coach Bill Walsh's team to a familiar place—Super Bowl XXIII at Miami's Joe Robbie Stadium on January 22, 1989. Despite its earlier problems, many expected San Francisco (10-6 during the regular season) to win handily against Cincinnati (12-4). The Bengals were coached by one of Walsh's former assistants, Sam Wyche, so fans expected a shootout.

Wrong on both counts. Instead of a 49ers' runaway, the Bengals hung tough, and instead of a high-scoring affair, the teams traded field goals for nearly three quarters in one of the hardest-hitting Super Bowls. After Jim Breech kicked a 40-yard field goal to give Cincinnati a 16-13 lead late in the fourth quarter, an upset seemed imminent.

That feeling only grew stronger when a penalty on the ensuing kickoff put the 49ers back to their 8-yard line with 3:10 left. Pressure? Not for Joe Montana, just two years removed from career-threatening back surgery and two months removed from nearly losing his starting job to Steve Young.

The 49ers' quarterback coolly led his team down the field, completing 8 of 9 passes for 97 yards. The key play on the drive came on second-and-20 from the Bengals' 45 with 1:17 remaining, when Montana completed a 27-yard strike to Jerry Rice crossing over the middle.

Montana's 8-yard pass to Roger Craig put  San Francisco at the Bengals' 10-yard line with 39 seconds left. Cincinnati expected a pass to Rice. Walsh instead called for Montana to look for Craig. When Craig was covered, Montana came back to the middle and fired a 10-yard touchdown pass to John Taylor (his only reception in the game) with 34 seconds remaining.

The pass completed the 49ers' 92-yard march, the most famous drive in Super Bowl history, and gave San Francisco a 20-16 victory. Montana finished with 23 completions in 36 attempts for 357 yards.

John Taylor's only reception in Super Bowl XXIII gave the 49ers a 20-16 victory.

THE GREATEST COMEBACK
January 3, 1993

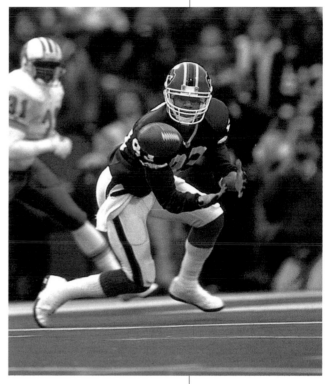

Could it get any worse?

The Buffalo Bills asked that question at halftime of their 1992 AFC Wild Card Game. Buffalo, playing at home, trailed Houston 28-3. And it got worse. Early in the third quarter, Houston safety Bubba McDowell returned an interception 58 yards for a touchdown. The Oilers led 35-3 and seemed ready to make plans to face the Steelers in the next playoff round.

The Bills, however, would not go gently into that good night. The two-time defending AFC champions scored 4 touchdowns in a span of 6 minutes 54 seconds, beginning with Kenneth Davis's 1-yard run midway through the third period. A successful onside kick and an interception keyed the Bills' explosion, which cut Houston's advantage to 35-31.

In the fourth quarter, Buffalo took its first lead on a 17-yard pass from Frank Reich (his fourth touchdown pass) to Andre Reed. The shell-shocked Oilers managed to drive to a tying field goal with 12 seconds remaining to force overtime, but that only staved off the inevitable. Early in the extra period, Buffalo cornerback Nate Odomes intercepted a pass from Houston's Warren Moon. Three plays later, Steve Christie kicked a 32-yard field goal to give Buffalo a 41-38 victory and complete the greatest comeback in NFL history.

Reich, playing in place of injured Jim Kelly, completed 21 of 34 passes for 289 yards. Reed had 8 receptions for 136 yards and 3 scores. Moon completed 36 of 50 passes for 371 yards and 4 touchdowns.

Andre Reed and the Bills made history with a comeback from 32 points behind.

NO LEAD IS SAFE
While attending Maryland, Frank Reich also led the greatest comeback in college football history. He rallied the Terrapins from a 31-0 halftime deficit to a 42-40 victory over Miami in 1984.

FINALLY!
John Elway played on three losing teams (Super Bowls XXI, XXII, and XXIV) before getting a chance to hoist the Vince Lombardi Trophy.

Running back Terrell Davis (30) shredded the Green Bay Packers' defense for 157 rushing yards and 3 touchdowns.

SUPER BOWL XXXII
January 25, 1998

"The Pack Is Back," or so everyone assumed before Super Bowl XXXII. The Green Bay Packers were poised to claim their second consecutive title. They entered the game favored by nearly 2 touchdowns against the Denver Broncos, a team known for Super Bowl pratfalls.

Denver had been outscored 163-50 while losing games XII, XXI, XXII, and XXIV. Many Broncos fans cringed at the thought of another big-game blowout. This team, however, had something the previous Broncos squads had lacked: a power-running attack.

Specifically, the Broncos had Terrell Davis. They also had nothing to lose, and on January 25, 1998, at San Diego's Qualcomm Stadium, they played like it.

Initially, the game went according to script. Green Bay took the opening kickoff and drove swiftly to a touchdown. Denver answered with Davis, who ran for a tying score, then turned loose its blitz to produce 2 turnovers, which led to 10 points and a 17-7 second-quarter lead.

Green Bay cut that lead to 17-14 before halftime, then tied the game at 17 in the third quarter. At that point, Davis, who sat out the second quarter with a severe migraine, took over. He carried 8 times on a 92-yard drive, a march that also included a headlong dive on an 8-yard run by quarterback John Elway for a key first down. Davis finished it with a 1-yard touchdown run to give Denver a 24-17 lead.

Early in the fourth quarter, Green Bay tied the game on Brett Favre's third touchdown pass, a 13-yard completion to Antonio Freeman. The teams traded punts until Denver took over at the Packers' 49 with 3:27 remaining. Elway's 23-yard pass to Howard Griffith and Davis's 17-yard run set up Davis's winning score on a 1-yard run with 1:45 remaining. The Packers mounted a last charge, but Denver linebacker John Mobley knocked away Favre's pass on fourth down from the Broncos' 31.

Davis, who set a Super Bowl record by running for 3 touchdowns, gained 157 yards on 30 carries and was named the game's MVP.

SUPER BOWL XXXIV
January 30, 2000

Super Bowl XXXIV in the Georgia Dome featured the unlikeliest of teams and the unlikeliest of heroes.

The St. Louis Rams, one of the NFL's least successful franchises during the 1990s, sprang from 4-12 in 1998 to 13-3 in 1999. Much of the improvement could be attributed to Kurt Warner, a second-string quarterback who became the starter when Trent Green suffered a season-ending knee injury in the preseason. Warner, just five years removed from working as a stock clerk in a supermarket, went on to compile one of the greatest seasons by a passer in NFL history.

On the other side were the Tennessee Titans, the NFL's vagabonds. The Titans had been the Houston Oilers until 1997, when the franchise moved to Tennessee. While they waited for their home stadium to be built in Nashville, the team first played in Memphis, then at Vanderbilt University. They finally found a home in 1999, their first year as the Titans.

They reached the Super Bowl thanks in large part to the "Music City Miracle," a cross-field lateral that Kevin Dyson turned into a game-winning 75-yard kickoff return in the final seconds of an AFC Wild Card Game.

The Titans almost pulled another miracle against the Rams. Despite surrendering 294 total yards, the Titans trailed only 9-0 at halftime. That deficit increased to 16-0 after the Rams' first possession of the second half, when Warner finally got St. Louis into the end zone with a 9-yard touchdown pass to Torry Holt.

That's when running back Eddie George and quarterback Steve McNair ignited Tennessee's offense. Behind George's running and McNair's running and passing, the Titans reeled off 16 points in less than 14 minutes, tying the game on Al Del Greco's 43-yard field goal with 2:12 remaining.

The Rams needed only one play to reclaim the lead. Warner (who finished with a record 414 passing yards and the MVP trophy) went deep along the right sideline for a streaking Isaac Bruce. The receiver slowed to catch the underthrown pass (Warner had been hit as he threw), broke a tackle, then cut to the middle of the field and raced to the end zone to complete a 73-yard touchdown pass.

Trailing 23-16 with 1:54 left, the gritty Titans drove from their 12 to the Rams' 10. The key play came on third-and-5 from the Rams' 26, when McNair made a remarkable escape from two Rams defenders and fired a 16-yard pass to Dyson with six seconds left.

That gave Tennessee one shot at tying the game. The Titans' outside receivers ran into the end zone, and Dyson ran underneath. McNair delivered a strike to Dyson, who only had one man to beat. But Rams linebacker Mike Jones tackled Dyson 1 yard short of the goal line for the most dramatic finish in Super Bowl history.

The Titans came up 1 yard short when Mike Jones tackled Kevin Dyson on the game's last play.

RECORD SETTER
Rams quarterback Kurt Warner, in his first year as a starter, broke the single-game Super Bowl record for passing yardage that had been set by Joe Montana.

25
Most
Important
Events

THE FIRST PROFESSIONAL

The Allegheny Athletic Association (AAA) wanted to beat its arch rival (the Pittsburgh Athletic Club, or PAC) so badly on November 12, 1892, that it did something unheard-of, at least in polite circles—the club paid someone to play football.

Former Yale All-America guard William (Pudge) Heffelfinger earned $500 that day, plus $25 for expenses. For AAA, it proved to be money well spent. In the first half, Heffelfinger jarred the ball from a PAC player, picked up the fumble, and raced 35 yards for a touchdown (worth 4 points in those days), the only score in AAA's 4-0 victory.

Certainly, others before Heffelfinger had been paid to play football, but always in secret because of public disdain for professional athletes. The AAA's official ledger for that game (left) represents the first proof of payment to an athlete, thereby making Heffelfinger the first acknowledged pro football player.

THE NFL IS FORMED

By 1920, pro football never had been more popular. Pro teams proliferated throughout the Midwest, but without much organization.

Consequently, teams poached players, collegians often also played for pro teams, and scheduling games proved to be a nightmare. Competition for players sent costs spiraling and threatened the survival of the sport.

Against that backdrop, seven men, representing four Ohio teams, gathered in Ralph Hay's Hupmobile showroom on August 20, 1920. All agreed on the necessity of a league, one that would provide structure and enforce the rules. Several earlier attempts had failed, but, undeterred, they instructed Hay to contact the owners of the other pro football teams and organize the new league.

Four weeks later, on September 17, 1920, representatives from 10 teams gathered at Hay's showroom. Limited seating forced several members of the group to sit on automobile fenders and running boards while they formed the American Professional Football Association (APFA), which had a stated goal of "raising the standard of professional football."

Club owners established a $100 fee to join the league, although no team ever paid. They elected legendary athlete Jim Thorpe as the league's first president, more for the publicity his name generated than for his administrative

Jim Thorpe, more athlete than administrator, was APFA president.

skills (he spent his only year in office playing for the Canton Bulldogs).

Two years later, the APFA changed its name to the National Football League. Eighty years later, it is the most popular sports league in America.

HALAS TAKES OVER THE BEARS

The group of representatives who gathered for the second meeting in Ralph Hay's Hupmobile showroom included George Halas, who represented the Decatur Staleys. Halas already enjoyed celebrity status for his athletic skills—he had been a football star at the University of Illinois and played briefly for baseball's New York Yankees in 1919.

He came to Hay's showroom as the player-coach of the Staleys, which were sponsored by A.E. Staley of Decatur, Illinois. The players spent their days working in Staley's starch works, then headed for the field adjacent to the factory to practice. The Staleys (10-1-2) nearly won the APFA title in 1920.

Success on the football field, however, did not translate into financial success. Money woes forced A.E. Staley to offer the team to Halas, who had limited funds of his own. Staley agreed to sweeten the deal by throwing in $5,000 to retain the name Staleys for a year (the franchise was renamed the Bears in 1922). Halas concluded that he had to move the franchise to Chicago to succeed, so he brought in a partner (another player, Dutch Sternaman) to help swing the deal.

That proved fortuitous, not only for the Bears, but for the entire NFL. No other person had a more profound impact on professional football than Halas, who owned the franchise from 1921 until his death in 1983 (he bought out Sternaman in 1933). Along the way, he left his mark on the game as a player (he held the record for longest fumble return until 1972), coach (he won 324 games, second only to Don Shula in league history), and owner (among his innovations was the introduction of the NFL Championship Game).

The Bears, along with the Arizona Cardinals, are the only charter franchises still competing in the NFL.

George Halas: player, coach, and owner

It was a hot day, and we sat there drinking beer from buckets while we tried to plan the future of professional football.

George Halas

THE FIRST SEASON
The APFA began play in 1920 with 14 teams, each playing a different number of games. The owners gathered after the season and awarded the league title to the Akron Pros (8-0-3), the APFA's only undefeated team. The Pros almost were the league's only champion. The APFA had accomplished little, and the discouraged owners were ready to give up. But Joe Carr, manager of the Columbus Panhandles, urged them to give the league another year. The owners agreed, and promptly elected Carr as president. He would prove instrumental to the NFL's development.

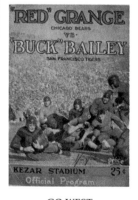

Green Bay Saves The Packers

Franchises came and went during the NFL's early years; the departed included the league's first champion (Akron Pros) and the league's first dominant team (Canton Bulldogs, the 1922 and 1923 champion). Only 4 (Bears, Cardinals, Giants, and Packers) of the 49 teams that competed during the 1920s still exist.

The Packers' inclusion in the four survivors is testament to a city's love affair with its team. They began play in 1919, funded by the Indian Packing Company, and joined the APFA in 1921. But the team struggled financially, and the league canceled the franchise after one season because the Packers used college players.

Coach Earl (Curly) Lambeau managed to persuade the owners to reinstate the franchise with him as part owner, but the Packers fared no better financially in 1922. Inclement weather dampened attendance, and even rain insurance (guaranteed gate receipts in the event of rain) did not help. The insurance company refused to pay because the official amount of precipitation fell one-hundredth of an inch short of that required by the policy.

The destitute Packers were headed for the scrap heap of history (along with the Pros, Bulldogs, and numerous other teams) until the community stepped in and made a game-saving play. Local business leaders reorganized the Packers as a nonprofit corporation, selling shares of stock for $5 each (fans who bought shares also received a season ticket).

The people of Green Bay rescued the Packers from another financial crisis in 1933, and, to this day, the club enjoys a unique status as the only publicly owned franchise in the NFL. The Packers also hold the distinction of most successful franchise in the NFL, having won 12 league titles.

The Galloping Ghost Turns Pro

The NFL's early days featured ongoing crises. Each threatened the league's existence, but the NFL somehow survived.

Red Grange (white jersey, at right) packed in spectators during a whirlwind barnstorming tour.

The league persevered in 1925 thanks largely to the arrival of Harold (Red) Grange, the "Galloping Ghost." Grange earned his nickname at the University of Illinois, where defenders trying to tackle him often wound up grasping air instead. He became the most celebrated college football player of his day (or any day), equal in stature to baseball's Babe Ruth or boxing's Jack Dempsey.

While fans came out in droves to see college games (nearly 73,000 had witnessed Grange's last appearance at Illinois), the public still viewed pro football with some disdain. That changed when Bears owner George Halas signed Grange, who made his pro debut on Thanksgiving Day. A packed house of 36,000 at Wrigley Field—then the largest crowd in pro football history—watched the Cardinals and Bears battle to a scoreless tie in the regular-season finale.

Then the fun started. The contract that Grange's agent, C.C. Pyle, signed with Halas called for the Bears to embark on a national barnstorming tour, headlined by Grange. The Bears played eight games in 12 days, from St. Louis to the East Coast and back to Chicago.

No game proved more meaningful than the stop in New York, where 73,000 fans turned out to see the Bears play the Giants at the Polo Grounds. Grange's appearance amounted to a life preserver for Tim Mara's Giants, who were drowning in a sea of red ink during their inaugural season.

After that first tour, Grange and the Bears took a week off, then embarked on another whirlwind excursion, this time in the South and West. Nine games in 17 days were to follow, highlighted by a stop in Los Angeles that drew 75,000 fans.

Though Grange was elected to the Pro Football Hall of Fame as a running back and defensive back, he always will be remembered more as the man who saved pro football in New York, and as the man who helped the sport gain national acceptance.

'THE FIRST CHAMPIONSHIP GAME'

During the NFL's first 12 years (1920-1931), the team with the best winning percentage claimed the league title. There was no such thing as a championship game.

Complications arose in 1932, when the Chicago Bears (6-1-6) and Portsmouth Spartans (6-1-4) each posted an .857 winning percentage (tie games did not count in figuring percentage then) to share the top spot. Rather than having the owners vote to award the title, as they had done several times during the 1920s, the league office scheduled a tie-breaker playoff between the two teams, to be played December 18 in Chicago.

When a blizzard hit the Midwest in the week before the game, another innovation followed: indoor football. Bears owner George Halas moved the game from Wrigley Field to Chicago Stadium, where the Bears had played an exhibition game two years earlier.

Bears owner George Halas moved the 1932 tie-breaker game indoors to Chicago Stadium after a blizzard hit the city.

BEYOND COMPARE
As a runner, blocker, and tackler, Bronko Nagurski was one of the most versatile players of his day. His talents included passing and his signature play, in which he would fake a dive into the line, then drop back and pass. He used that play to win the 1932 title for Chicago.

The circus had just left town, leaving a floor covered in dirt. The arena could accommodate only an 80-yard field, which was surrounded by a fence three feet from the sideline. Officials adjusted by imposing a 20-yard penalty for crossing midfield (to simulate a regulation-length field), moving the goal posts to the goal line instead of the end line, and by utilizing inbounds lines (called "hashmarks"). When a play ended out of bounds, officials returned the ball to the nearest hashmark, so the offense would not be pressed against the sideline.

The teams battled to a scoreless tie until the fourth quarter, when the Bears' Bronko Nagurski tossed a 2-yard touchdown pass to Red Grange. The Spartans howled in protest, claiming that Nagurski had not been five yards behind the line, as required by the rules then. Portsmouth's protests proved futile, and Chicago added a safety to win 9-0.

The game's impact extended beyond merely determining the 1932 champion. The next year, Halas helped push through several new rules, and pro football finally forged an identity separate from the college game. Those changes permitted a forward pass to be thrown from anywhere behind the line of scrimmage and established hashmarks 10 yards from the inbounds line, so teams would no longer have to waste a play just to get the ball back to the middle of the field. In addition, the league moved the goal posts from the end line to the goal line.

The changes resulted in more wide-open play, more scoring, and more fans. One additional modification also proved propitious: The league divided into Eastern and Western Divisions, with the winner of each division advancing to the NFL Championship Game, first played in 1933.

PRO VERSUS COLLEGIANS

Though college football still ruled, the NFL gained prestige with the introduction of the Chicago College All-Star Game in 1934. The game, played every summer at Chicago's Soldier Field, matched the defending league champion against the best college players.

In its infancy, the Chicago College All-Star Game elevated the NFL in the eyes of fans by placing it on par with the more popular college game. In later years, after the league had gained national acceptance, the contest became a preseason special for football fans and a vehicle to raise money for worthy causes. The Chicago College All-Star Game attracted huge crowds during most of its 42-year run (1934-1973, 1975-76) while raising more than $4 million for charity. The game was discontinued when it became clear that college players—even a team of all-stars—were overmatched by professionals.

THE BIRTH OF THE DRAFT

Every year, a new crop of college players would enter the NFL, and every year, the rich teams got richer. So Philadelphia Eagles owner Bert Bell hit upon an idea: Why not have teams draft college players in inverse order of their finish in the standings, so the worst teams would get the earliest picks? That way, poor teams could improve.

The other owners agreed, and, in February, 1936, they gathered at Philadelphia's Ritz-Carlton Hotel for the first NFL draft. Unlike today's drafts, informality prevailed, as old friends chatted and Redskins owner George Preston Marshall serenaded the group,

Jay Berwanger, the first draft pick, chose not to play.

accompanied by Cardinals coach Jimmy Conzelman on the piano.

Bell's woeful Eagles had the first pick, and they selected University of Chicago halfback Jay Berwanger, then traded his rights to the Bears. Berwanger never played a down in the NFL (never even signed a contract), but his place in football history is secure: The first player picked in the NFL draft also won the first Heisman Trophy.

Today the draft is an event, spanning two days in April and nationally televised. For seven rounds (it has been as long as 30 rounds), teams restock rosters. Bell's original premise—that the worst teams pick first—remains, giving football fans in every city hope that this will be their team's year.

FIRST TELEVISED GAME

Football and television are perfectly suited, so it is only fitting that NFL games were among the first events broadcast.

On October 22, 1939, the Brooklyn Dodgers hosted the Philadelphia Eagles at Ebbets Field. Using only one camera, NBC transmitted the action to its Manhattan studio, which broadcast the game to the 1,000 or so television sets that existed, all in the New York City area.

Both television and the NFL have come a long way since. For Super Bowl XXXIV on January 30, 2000, ABC utilized 40 cameras while broadcasting the game to an estimated 43.6 million American households.

THE NFL GOES WEST

During the early decades of professional sports, teams were concentrated in the East and Midwest, where most Americans lived. Even as the population shifted West, no teams followed because traveling that far for a Sunday game would have required several days on a train, going and coming.

World War II changed that. Larger aircraft made cross-country travel a same-day trip rather than a three- to four-day event. In addition, many servicemen who passed through California on their way overseas returned to live there, dramatically increasing the westward population shift already underway.

Cleveland Rams owner Dan Reeves had been considering a move to the West Coast for some time. Despite the fact that the Rams had suspended operations in 1943 and had lost money in 1944, the other owners refused his request to move to Los Angeles, concerned about prohibitive travel costs.

The owners' attitude changed when the new All-America Football Conference announced plans to put a team in Los Angeles. After the Cleveland Rams won the 1945 NFL title—and Reeves lost another $50,000—NFL owners voted 8-0 to grant Reeves's request. Home to perennial college power Southern California, Los Angeles long had been a football bastion, and the city welcomed the Rams with open arms. The National Football League finally lived up to its name.

Los Angeles fans welcomed the Rams and the NFL to the West Coast with open arms.

L.A. STORY
Los Angeles experienced pro football before the Rams arrived in 1946. Red Grange played there in 1926, during his second barnstorming tour, and the city hosted three Pro Bowls in 1939 and 1940. In those days, the Pro Bowl matched the league champion against a team of NFL all-stars, and it was sponsored by the *Los Angeles Times* (see program above).

TRAIL BLAZER
Several African-Americans played in the NFL during the 1920s, most notably Fritz Pollard (above). Pollard played halfback at Brown, where he became only the second African-American to be named to Walter Camp's All-America team. He spent six seasons in the NFL, also serving as player-coach in 1921 and 1925. He was the first African-American coach in professional sports.

BREAKING THE BARRIER
After a 13-year absence, African-Americans returned to the NFL in 1946 when the Los Angeles Rams signed Woody Strode (above) and Kenny Washington. Both were hometown heroes, having starred at local high schools and at UCLA. Strode, 32, played 10 games in his only NFL season, catching 4 passes for 37 yards.

THE COLOR LINE IS BROKEN—AGAIN

Unlike baseball, the NFL had African-American players from its earliest days, including famed actor, orator, and civil rights activist Paul Robeson (1921-22). Fritz Pollard became the first black coach in any pro sport when he led the Akron Pros to a third-place finish in 1921.

From 1933-1945, however, the league excluded black players. That injustice ended in 1946—a year before Jackie Robinson's major league baseball debut—when the Rams signed Kenny Washington (pictured above) and Woody Strode. Soon after, the Cleveland Browns of the All-America Football Conference signed Marion Motley and Bill Willis.

Washington played three seasons for the Rams and Strode played one, while Motley and Willis enjoyed Hall of Fame careers with the Browns. Their arrival dissolved the color barrier forever in pro football.

THE RAMS GROW HORNS

The Rams went Hollywood in 1946 when they moved from Cleveland to Los Angeles. The rest of the league soon followed, thanks to Rams running back Fred Gehrke.

Early NFL teams put a rather drab-looking product out on the field, with monochromatic uniforms and unadorned helmets. With all the players dressed in undistinctive gear, the team identity of players was difficult to determine in pileups.

That changed when Gehrke, a former art student, drew horns on a Rams' helmet. The Rams liked his handiwork so much that they adopted his design for 1948.

Every NFL team (except for the Browns, to this day) eventually adopted unique helmet logos, giving each a marketable identity and helping to raise the league's visibility among sports fans. Gehrke played seven seasons in the NFL and scored 24 touchdowns, but easily his most lasting contribution was as an innovator in fashion design.

Fred Gehrke is remembered more for his artistic touch than his football talent.

THE PRO BOWL CATCHES ON

Today, the Pro Bowl is a popular fixture, the last football game of every season and a chance for fans to see the best players from each conference compete on the same field. But the game has not always enjoyed such lofty status. At first, from 1939-1942, the league champion annually faced a team of NFL all-stars. The game disappeared during World War II because of travel restrictions and too few players.

After the war ended, however, the NFL boomed, and, flush with talented players, the league decided to revive the Pro Bowl after the 1950 season. All-stars from the American and National Conferences played each other in a game sponsored by the *Los Angeles Times*. The Los Angeles Memorial Coliseum hosted the game for 22 consecutive years (1951-1972). The Pro Bowl then rotated among sites until finding a permanent home in Hawaii, where it has been played since 1980.

Pro Bowl week now includes a variety of televised sidelights, and the game has become an annual sellout.

THE NFL ON NATIONAL TELEVISION

A long touchdown pass in the fourth quarter breaks a tie, and the Rams hang on to win the game and the title. That not only describes Super Bowl XXXIV, it also describes the 1951 NFL Championship Game, the first pro football game to be nationally televised.

The DuMont Network broadcast the game after paying $75,000 for the rights. The 57,522 fans who attended the game at the Los Angeles Coliseum and the millions more who watched at home were treated to an exciting rematch of the 1950 title game, which the Cleveland Browns had won 30-28 on a last-minute field goal by Lou Groza.

The Rams avenged their defeat of the year before when sure-handed Tom Fears took a pass from Norm Van Brocklin and sped downfield for a 73-yard touchdown that gave Los Angeles a 24-17 victory.

A sign of the times: Winning players earned $2,108 apiece, losers $1,483.

THE 'GREATEST GAME EVER PLAYED'

TELEVISION TIME OUT
In the 1958 NFL title game, NBC lost its broadcast feed at the end of regulation. Like a good book with the last chapter torn out, viewers were about to miss the best part. But the field judge extended the time out, giving the network time to correct the technical problem.

On December 28, 1958, many Americans discovered pro football, and neither the game nor the country has been the same since. On that day, the Baltimore Colts played the New York Giants in the NFL Championship Game at Yankee Stadium. Although the NFL had been on television from the beginning, and the title game had been nationally telecast since 1951, no other event had a greater impact on the league than this one.

Several factors helped make it the "Greatest Game Ever Played." First, the seesaw battle provided gripping drama. The Colts and Giants delivered all that football has to offer, including the first overtime period in NFL history. And like all epic theater, the game ended in dramatic fashion, with Alan Ameche barreling into the end zone to give the Colts a 23-17 victory.

THE 'COMPROMISE' NFL COMMISSIONER

When Bert Bell died after suffering a heart attack at an Eagles-Steelers game in 1959, it left the NFL with a giant vacancy. Bell had been commissioner since 1946, and in 13 years he had guided the league out of uncertainty and into an era of television-driven popularity. Suddenly, with a rival league (the American Football League) about to form and expansion looming, the NFL lacked proven leadership.

In January, 1960, the 12 club owners met in Miami Beach, Florida, to settle the issue. The old guard, led by Redskins owner George Preston Marshall and Colts owner Carroll Rosenbloom, favored NFL treasurer Austin Gunsel, the acting commissioner. Gunsel, however, did not have enough charisma to suit a rival bloc that pushed for San Francisco 49ers attorney Marshall Leahy.

Election required a three-fourths majority (9 of 12 votes), but neither side would budge during seven grueling days and 22 ballots. Finally, two of the league's most respected figures—the Giants' Wellington Mara and Cleveland's Paul Brown—hit upon a solution. They nominated Pete Rozelle, the articulate and personable general manager of the Los Angeles

> **"**
> *If God Almighty came down from Heaven and agreed to serve as commissioner, you'd [still] vote for Leahy.*
> **"**
>
> *Carroll Rosenbloom*

Second, the teams featured numerous legends—15 future Pro Football Hall of Fame members either played or coached in the game that day. Finally, and most importantly, television brought all of this drama into America's living rooms.

Great games had been played before, but never had so many viewers seen the action. The rectangular field proved perfectly suited to the rectangular screen. Thanks to television, pro football made millions of new fans. That day marked the birth of the modern NFL.

Bears owner George Halas (far left) and Redskins owner George Marshall (second from right) finally found common ground with the selection of Pete Rozelle (center).

Rams, a choice that both sides could accept despite his youth (33) and relative inexperience.

On January 26, on the twenty-third ballot, the weary NFL owners elected Alvin (Pete) Rozelle as their new commissioner. Colts owner Carroll Rosenbloom gave him the news in the hotel men's room. Rozelle himself expressed concerns about his lack of qualifications for the job, but Brown comforted the young chief by telling him, "You can grow into the job."

Brown's words proved prophetic. During his three-decade tenure (1960-1989), Rozelle's leadership helped transform the NFL into a household name, not only in America but around the world. He is widely recognized as the most influential league leader in the history of pro sports.

SHARING THE WEALTH

Before Pete Rozelle became commissioner, each team negotiated a separate television deal, and the disparities in market size led to disparities in television revenue. If that situation persisted, the league would cease to be competitive because the large-market teams would dominate.

Rozelle recognized that fact, and he recognized that when it came to the NFL's television rights, the whole amounted to much more than the sum of its parts. In other words, the league could maximize revenues by selling its television rights collectively to a network. At the same time, the NFL would insure the competitiveness of small-market teams by equally distributing the proceeds.

After some cajoling, Rozelle convinced the large-market teams to give up their lucrative television deals for the good of the league. Armed with their acquiescence, he signed a contract with CBS in 1961.

Rozelle's plan almost went awry when a federal court invalidated the contract on antitrust grounds. But the commissioner pleaded the league's case to a New York congressman, who introduced a bill to legalize single-network contracts for sports leagues. Congress passed the bill, President Kennedy signed it, and in January of 1962, CBS secured the rights to all NFL games in exchange for $4.65 million annually.

Today each team receives an equal share of the league's television contracts (amounting to tens of millions of dollars annually), which helps put the Packers of Green Bay (population 96,466) on an equal footing with the Jets and Giants from New York (population 8.6 million).

THE AFL-NFL MERGER

"The Foolish Club" is what the original eight AFL owners called themselves. Foolish for thinking they could compete against the established NFL. Foolish for spending all that money on such a hopeless pursuit.

The American Football League came about because of Lamar Hunt, a Texas businessman. Hunt wanted an NFL franchise for Dallas, but his attempt to buy the Cardinals failed and the league denied his request for an expansion team. So he created a league of his own.

Eight teams, including Hunt's Dallas Texans, began play in 1960. The Boston Patriots,

Lamar Hunt, Ralph Wilson, Wayne Valley, and William Sullivan were members of the Foolish Club.

Buffalo Bills, Denver Broncos, Houston Oilers, Los Angeles Chargers, New York Titans, and Oakland Raiders were the other teams. The AFL soon became known for its wide-open play, and after signing a new television contract with NBC in 1965, the league posed a viable threat to the NFL.

By 1966, the bidding for college players threatened the solvency of both leagues. NFL Commissioner Pete Rozelle authorized Dallas Cowboys executive Tex Schramm to begin merger talks with Hunt, now the owner of the Kansas City Chiefs (he had relocated his franchise in 1963).

Previous merger attempts had failed, but this time Schramm offered a marriage of relative equals (earlier proposals had called for the elimination or transfer of some AFL teams). After two months of secret negotiations, Schramm and Hunt reached an agreement, which Rozelle announced on June 8, 1966.

The plan called for the AFL and NFL to merge into a 26-team league in 1970, divided into two 13-team conferences. The leagues would hold a combined draft of college players beginning in 1967. The merger also called for the nine AFL teams to pay the NFL $18 million over 20 years.

For the NFL, the merger proved to be the springboard for another explosion of popularity. For the "Foolish Club," the merger amounted to the realization of an impossible dream.

THE SUPER BOWL IS BORN

Though the AFL-NFL merger would not occur until 1970, the merger agreement called for a game between the league champions, beginning after the 1966 season. So on January 15, 1967, the AFL-champion Kansas City Chiefs met the NFL-champion Green Bay Packers in the first AFL-NFL World Championship Game (above).

That unwieldy title did not last. The media quickly coined the term "Super Bowl," inspired by an offhand remark from Chiefs owner Lamar Hunt. That first Super Bowl is unrecognizable by today's standards. Tickets sold for $6 to $12, and many of them went begging (only 61,946 attended the game in the 94,000-seat Los Angeles Coliseum), the only nonsellout in Super Bowl history.

Both leagues' networks (CBS for the NFL and NBC for the AFL) televised the game, though not to Los Angeles, where the game was blacked out. Each team used its official league ball on offense (Spalding for the AFL and Wilson for the NFL).

The Chiefs made it competitive for one half, trailing only 14-10 at intermission. Green Bay dominated the second half, though, scoring all 21 points to run away with a 35-10 victory.

GET YOUR PROGRAM! The NFL produced the Super Bowl I program (above) in just 10 days. The program sold for $1 at the game. Today it sells for many times that, thanks to its scarcity. Apparently no one thought to keep any film, either: No complete video tape of the game survives.

NAMATH'S GUARANTEED VICTORY

The first two Super Bowls were less than compelling. As expected, the older NFL dominated both games. More specifically, the Green Bay Packers pounded two overmatched AFL teams.

Super Bowl III—the first officially called a Super Bowl—figured to be an even greater mismatch. Many considered the Baltimore Colts, the NFL's representative, one of the greatest teams in history. Baltimore came to Miami with a 15-1 record, including a 34-0 rout of Cleveland in the NFL title game.

The Colts' opponent, the New York Jets (11-3), had posted the third-best record in the AFL, then barely squeezed by the Oakland Raiders in the AFL Championship Game. Odds makers gave them little chance against the Colts, who were 18- to 21-point favorites.

Super Bowl III had more than just league pride riding on its outcome. Several influential owners believed that AFL teams clearly could not compete against the NFL. Consequently, one postmerger plan called for the AFL teams to be dispersed among the NFL teams, rather than maintaining the AFL-NFL rivalry. According to that plan, the league champion would be determined by the NFL title game (played at one team's home rather than a neutral site) and the Super Bowl would end after the fourth contest, scheduled for January, 1970.

Just when the Super Bowl's days seemed numbered, an unlikely savior arrived. Quarterback Joe Namath (left) already had attracted considerable attention, with his long hair, distinctive white shoes, flamboyant lifestyle, and the huge contract he signed with the Jets in 1965. Broadway Joe and the Jets liked to have a good time, providing the perfect contrast to the button-down Colts, who were all business.

The Namath persona sometimes obscured his prodigious talent, something the Colts may have forgotten while they steamed over his comments. None of Namath's statements produced more froth than the one he offered three days before the game, at a banquet for the Miami Touchdown Club. After a fan declared the Colts were going to kill the Jets, Namath responded, "We're going to win. I guarantee it."

Namath had broken the golden rule of sports: Never rile your opponent before the game. Namath, though, had simply put a voice to what the Jets were thinking after watching film of the Colts and quietly preparing for a game almost everyone expected them to lose.

The rest is history. On Sunday, January 12, 1969, the Jets came out playing solid football, and the Colts came out making mistakes. Both followed the script until the end. With Namath calling almost all of the plays at the line, New York moved the ball methodically down the field, building a 16-0 lead.

The Colts mounted a last charge, but scored only a touchdown in New York's 16-7 victory, which ended with the indelible image of Namath leaving the field with his index finger raised to indicate that the Jets were number one. He had delivered on his guarantee.

The greatest upset in sports history put the Super Bowl on the map, prompting *The New York Times* to declare, "Because of what Joe Namath accomplished in the Super Bowl yesterday, pro football will never be the same again."

MONDAY NIGHT FOOTBALL

In the world of football, high schools own Fridays, colleges own Saturdays, and the pros own Sundays. What about Monday? That belonged to sitcoms, variety shows, and dramas, at least until 1970.

Monday nights changed forever that year, thanks to NFL Commissioner Pete Rozelle and ABC Sports president Roone Arledge. Rozelle wanted to attract more women to the sport, while ABC, the number-three network, just wanted something to put on the air.

So, on September 21, *Monday Night Football* debuted with the Cleveland Browns defeating the New York Jets 31-21 under the lights of Cleveland Municipal Stadium. Few expected the show to last more than a season. Instead, it became a national phenomenon. Bars set up big-screen televisions to accommodate the crowds, the announcers (especially Howard Cosell) became national figures, and teams lobbied for a chance to appear in the NFL's showcase game.

Monday Night Football still is running strong. The show completed its thirtieth season in 1999, the second-longest tenure for a prime-time show.

America spent its Monday nights with Don Meredith (left), Howard Cosell (center), and Frank Gifford.

A SUPER BOWL TV RECORD

Fifteen years after the first Super Bowl—which inspired as much curiosity and indifference as passion—the game had become a national holiday. Police reported a drop in crime and many shops closed on Super Sunday, all because America gathered around the television.

That never was more evident than on January 24, 1982, when nearly half the televisions in the nation tuned in to Super Bowl XVI, featuring the San Francisco 49ers and Cincinnati Bengals. The game attracted a Nielsen rating of 49.1, the highest ever for a sports event.

Later Super Bowls would post even gaudier numbers. An estimated 138.5 million Americans watched the Dallas Cowboys play the Pittsburgh Steelers in Super Bowl XXX, making it history's most-watched television program.

Super Bowl XVI earned a Nielsen rating of 49.1.

> "
> *If Jesus were alive today, He would be at the Super Bowl.*
> "
>
> *Norman Vincent Peale*

THE NFL GOES INTERNATIONAL

By the mid-1980s, public opinion surveys consistently showed that pro football had become America's favorite sport. Secure at home, the NFL looked for new territory to conquer overseas.

The international expedition began with the first American Bowl, played August 3, 1986, at London's Wembley Stadium. More than 80,000 British fans discovered "American football" while watching the defending champion Chicago Bears defeat the Dallas Cowboys 17-6 in a preseason contest.

That proved to be only the beginning. The American Bowl soon became an annual event at Wembley Stadium, and the series later expanded to include games in Tokyo, Berlin, and Barcelona, among other cities. In 1991-92, the NFL's World League became the first professional sports league to operate weekly on two separate continents.

In 1995, the World League evolved into NFL Europe, featuring six European teams battling for the right to play in the World Bowl. The league not only brings American football to Europe, it also serves as a farm system for NFL teams. One such product: Super Bowl XXXIV MVP Kurt Warner.

AN AFRICAN-AMERICAN COACH

In 1921, Fritz Pollard, a back for the Akron Pros, served as co-coach and helped guide the team to an 8-3-1 record and third place in the league. (He also coached the club in 1925). After that, the NFL did not have an African-American head coach for more than 60 years.

That wrong finally ended October 3, 1989, when Art Shell became the first African-American head coach of the modern era. Shell had excellent credentials: He had been a Hall of Fame tackle for 15 seasons (1968-1982) with the Raiders, then served as an assistant coach with the club for six years.

Raiders coach Art Shell

the club for six years. He took over a 1-3 Raiders team in 1989 and turned it into a playoff contender, then guided the club to the AFC West title in 1990.

Shell led the Raiders to a 54-38 regular-season record and three playoff berths during his six seasons as coach. He also opened the door for other African-American head coaches, including Minnesota's Dennis Green and Tampa Bay's Tony Dungy.

LABOR PEACE

The NFL's increasing popularity led to increasingly contentious labor negotiations between the owners and players, including three work stoppages in 13 years (1974-1987).

The players wanted free agency. The owners feared skyrocketing payrolls and potentially disastrous consequences. A court decision brought the matter to a head, and, in 1993, the two sides reached a compromise: The players got free agency and a guaranteed percentage of revenues, and the owners got a salary cap.

This agreement proved so successful that it has been extended to 2005, and the NFL finished the 1990s as the only pro sports league without a work stoppage in the decade.

INDEX

PHOTOGRAPHY CREDITS

(Legend: T=top, B=bottom, L=left, M=middle, R=right, TL=top left, TR= top right, ML=middle left, MR=middle right, BL=bottom left, BR=bottom right, a=above, b=below)

Page 1: Bob Rosato; **2TL**: Michael Burr; **2TR**: Manny Rubio; **2BL**: NFL Photos; **2BR**: George Rose; **3TL**: George Rose; **3TR**: Fred Kaplan; **3ML**: NFL Photos; **3MR(a)**: George Brace; **3MR(b)**: Associated Press; **3 (All Others)**: NFL Photos; **5**: Robert Riger; **6-7**: Peter Read Miller; **8L**: NFL Photos; **8R**: Vernon Biever; **9**: Fred Kaplan; **10**: Tony Tomsic; **11**: NFL Photos; **12TL**: John G. Zimmerman; **12BL**: Philadelphia Eagles; **12R**: NFL Photos; **13**: NFL Photos; **14**: Tony Tomsic; **15**: Pete Groh; **16**: Manny Rubio; **17**: Tony Tomsic; **18**: Dan Rubin; **19L**: Dick Raphael; **19R**: NFL Photos; **20**: Tony Tomsic; **21**: Lou Witt; **22TL**: Tony Tomsic; **22BL**: NFL Photos; **22BR**: Fred Roe; **23**: John McDonough; **24**: Darryl Norenberg; **25**: Alvin Chung; **26**: NFLP/Kevin Terrell; **27T**: Todd Rosenberg; **27B**: James Flores; **28**: Pro Football Hall of Fame; **29**: Tony Tomsic; **30**: NFL Photos; **31L**: Jim Turner; **31R**: John Biever; **32L**: Vernon Biever; **32R**: Tony Tomsic; **33**: Rich Pilling; **34L**: NFL Photos; **34R**: Carl Skalak; **35**: Peter Read Miller; **36T**: NFL Photos; **36B**: Vernon Biever; **37**: Daniel Rubin; **38T**: NFL Photos; **38B**: Pro Football Hall of Fame; **39**: Malcolm Emmons; **40**: Ken Hardin; **41L**: Vic Stein; **41R**: George Gojkovich; **42T**: Vic Stein; **42B**: James Flores; **43**: Corky Trewin; **44**: Frank Rippon; **45**: NFL Photos; **46**: Al Messerschmidt; **47L**: NFL Photos; **47R**: NFL Photos; **48**: Tony Tomsic; **49**: Glenn James; **50**: Frank Rippon; **51T**: Frank Rippon; **51B**: NFLP/Dave Boss; **52**: Peter Brouillet; **53**: Darryl Norenberg; **54**: Frank Kuchirchuk; **55T**: George Gojkovich; **55B**: George Brace; **56**: Tony Tomsic; **57**: Pro Football Hall of Fame; **58TL**: NFL Photos; **58BR**: NFLP/Dave Boss; **59**: Carl Skalak; **60T**: James Flores; **60B**: Malcolm Emmons; **61**: Malcolm Emmons; **62**: Al Messerschmidt; **63**: George Rose; **64**: Steven Murphy; **65**: David Drapkin; **66**: Malcolm Emmons; **67L**: NFLP/Dave Boss; **67R**: NFLP/Dave Boss; **68**: Carl Skalak; **69L**: Mitchell Reibel; **69R**: Robert Skeoch; **70**: David Stluka; **71**: Malcolm Emmons; **72TL**: Malcolm Emmons; **72BL**: Dallas Cowboys; **72R**: Dan Rubin; **73**: Rich Pilling; **74**: Malcolm Emmons; **75**: Nate Fine; **76**: NFL Photos; **77T**: Dan Burns; **77B**: Rob Brown; **78L**: Pro Football Hall of Fame; **78R**: Frank Rippon; **79**: NFL Photos; **80**: Tony Tomsic; **81B**: Peter Read Miller; **81TR**: Malcolm Emmons; **82L**: NFL Photos; **82R**: NFL Photos; **83**: NFL Photos; **84**: Malcolm Emmons; **85L**: Scott Cunningham; **85R**: Allen Kee; **86**: Tony Tomsic; **87**: Peter Read Miller; **88**: Greg Crisp; **89**: Thearon Henderson; **92-93**: Vernon Biever; **94**: NFL Photos; **95**: United Press International; **96-97**: United Press International; **97B**: NFL Photos; **98TL**: NFL Photos; **98B**: Vic Stein; **99T**: Pro Football Hall of Fame; **99B**: NFL Photos; **100T**: Fred Roe; **100B**: NFL Photos; **101**: Vernon Biever; **102**: Fred Roe; **103**: NFLP/Dave Boss; **104**: NFL Photos; **105**: NFLP/Dave Boss; **106-107**: Fred Kaplan; **107TR**: NFL Photos; **107B**: Vernon Biever; **108**: The Allens; **109T**: Vernon Biever; **109B**: NFL Photos; **110**: NFL Photos; **111T**: Nate Fine; **111B**: Malcolm Emmons; **112T**: Nate Fine; **112B**: George Tiedemann; **113**: Rob Brown; **114T**: Al Messerschmidt; **114B**: John Biever; **115**: Greg Trott; **116T**: James D. Smith; **116B**: George Rose; **117**: George Rose; **118**: Todd Rosenberg; **119**: Joe Culliton; **120-121**: Manny Rubio; **122T**: NFL Photos; **122B**: Pro Football Hall of Fame; **123**: Pro Football Hall of Fame; **124TL**: World Wide Photo; **124BL**: Pro Football Hall of Fame; **124BR**: NFL Photos; **125**: World Wide Photo; **126BL**: NFL Photos; **126-127**: Pro Football Hall of Fame; **127TR**: Vernon Biever; **128**: John Biever; **129L**: Russ Reed; **129BR**: NBC; **130T**: Dick Raphael; **130B**: Randy Reed; **131**: NFL Photos; **132**: NFL Photos; **133TL**: Dallas Cowboys; **133TR**: NFL Photos; **133BR**: Dick Raphael; **134**: Lou Witt; **135T**: Nate Fine; **135BR**: Malcolm Emmons; **136**: Al Messerschmidt; **137**: Joe Kennedy/Los Angeles Times; **138T**: Pete Groh; **138BR**: Bob Rosato; **139T**: David Drapkin; **139B**: David Drapkin; **140TL**: Bob Rosato; **140B**: Al Messerschmidt; **141T**: NFLP/Kevin Terrell; **141BR**: Michael Zagaris; **142-143**: Pro Football Hall of Fame; **144L**: NFL Photos; **144R**: Pro Football Hall of Fame; **145**: NFL Photos; **146 (All)**: NFL Photos; **147T**: Pro Football Hall of Fame; **147B**: George Brace; **148**: Pro Football Hall of Fame; **149T**: Vic Stein; **149BR**: NFL Photos; **150TL**: NFL Photos; **150BL**: NFL Photos; **150R**: Vic Stein; **151T**: NFL Photos; **151B**: NFL Photos; **152-153**: Robert Riger; **153BR**: Associated Press; **154**: Ross Lewis; **155T**: Fred Roe; **155BR**: NFL Photos; **156T**: Darryl Norenberg; **156BL**: NFL Photos; **157TR**: John Biever; **157BL**: ABC Sports; **158L**: Al Messerschmidt; **158R**: NFL Photos.